POPULAR WILDFLOWERS

of Coastal British Columbia *and* Vancouver Island

NEIL L. JENNINGS

RMB

This book is dedicated to the memory of Bruce McKinnon,
beloved husband, son, brother, artist,
man for all seasons – a good man in a storm.
Too soon gone; sorely missed; fondly remembered.

Popular Wildflowers of Coastal British Columbia and Vancouver Island
Copyright © 2020 by Neil L. Jennings
First Edition

For information on purchasing bulk quantities of this book, or to
obtain media excerpts or invite the author to speak at an event,
please visit rmbooks.com and select the "Contact" tab.

RMB | Rocky Mountain Books Ltd.
rmbooks.com
@rmbooks
facebook.com/rmbooks

Cataloguing data available from Library and Archives Canada
ISBN 9781771603454 (paperback)
ISBN 9781771603461 (electronic)

All photographs are by the author unless otherwise noted.

Printed and bound in Canada

We would like to also take this opportunity to acknowledge the traditional territories
upon which we live and work. In Calgary, Alberta, we acknowledge the Niitsitapi
(Blackfoot) and the people of the Treaty 7 region in Southern Alberta, which includes
the Siksika, the Piikuni, the Kainai, the Tsuut'ina and the Stoney Nakoda First Nations,
including Chiniki, Bearpaw, and Wesley First Nations. The City of Calgary is also home
to Métis Nation of Alberta, Region III. In Victoria, British Columbia, we acknowledge the
traditional territories of the Lkwungen (Esquimalt, and Songhees), Malahat, Pacheedaht,
Scia'new, T'Sou-ke and W̱SÁNEĆ (Pauquachin, Tsartlip, Tsawout, Tseycum) peoples.

We acknowledge the financial support of the Government of Canada through the Canada
Book Fund and the Canada Council for the Arts, and of the province of British Columbia
through the British Columbia Arts Council and the Book Publishing Tax Credit.

Disclaimer

It is up to the users of this guidebook to acquire the necessary skills for safe experiences
and to exercise caution. The author and publisher of this guide accept no responsibility for
your actions or the results that occur from another's actions, choices, or judgments. If you
have any doubt as to the safety of any given plant, avoidance is the best course of action.

CONTENTS

Acknowledgements   vii

Introduction   viii

Territorial Range of Wildflowers   x

Red, Orange and Pink Flowers   1

White, Green and Brown Flowers   27

Blue and Purple Flowers   56

Yellow Flowers   70

Glossary   89

Index   93

About the Author   102

ACKNOWLEDGEMENTS

I owe a debt of gratitude to a number of family members who contributed to this book by their continuous encouragement and support. Particular appreciation goes to my wife, Linda, who accompanied me on many flower outings and allowed me frequent absences from other duties in favour of chasing blooming flowers. My children, and, I am happy to say, their children, all deserve mention as well, given that they were often seconded to tramp around with me and bring me home alive. Thanks also go to many friends who encouraged me in my projects and often went into the field with me, according me a level of patience that was above and beyond the call of duty. I also wish to especially thank (or perhaps blame) the now departed S. Don Cahoon, who often shamed me with my ignorance and convinced me to educate myself about the beauty that resides in fields of wildflowers.

INTRODUCTION

This book is intended to be a field guide for the amateur naturalist to the identification of wild flowering plants commonly found in the coastal areas of British Columbia, including Vancouver Island. This is not a book for scientists. It is for the curious traveller who wants to become acquainted with the flowers encountered during outings. The book differs from most other field guides in that it makes no assumption that the reader has any background in things botanical. It is also small enough to actually carry in the field and not be a burden. I believe most people want to be able to identify the flowers they encounter because this enriches their outdoor experience. Some might think it a difficult skill to perfect, but take heart and consider this: you can easily put names and faces together for several hundred family members, friends, acquaintances, movie stars, authors, business and world leaders, sports figures etc. Wildflower recognition is no different, and it need not be complicated.

For this book, the area of interest is loosely described as coastal British Columbia, Vancouver Island, Washington and Oregon, from coastal elevations eastward and upwards to the alpine community on the western side of the mountains.

The book does not cover all of the species of wildflowers and flowering shrubs that exist in the Pacific Northwest, but it does include a large representation of the more common floral communities that might be encountered in a typical day during the blooming season. No book that I am acquainted with covers all species in any region, and indeed if such a source existed, it would be too large to be easily carried. For example, it is estimated that in the Composite Family (Sunflowers) alone there are over 1,000 species in over 100 genera in the region. Obviously, space will not permit a discussion of all such species, nor would it be pertinent for the amateur naturalist. The region harbours a vast diversity of habitat. In fact, for its relative size, the region is said to have the greatest diversity of plant species of any comparable area in North America.

"Do you know what this flower is called?" is one of the most often asked questions when I meet people in the field. Hopefully, this book will enable the user to answer this question. Identification of the unknown species is based on comparison of the unknown plant with the photographs contained in the book, augmented by the narrative descriptions associated with the species pictured. In many instances the exact species will be apparent, while in other cases the reader will be led to plants that are similar to the unknown plant, thus providing a starting point for further investigation. For the purposes of this book, scientific jargon has been kept to a minimum. I have set out to produce the best photographic representations I could obtain, together with some information about the plant that the reader might find interesting, and that might assist the reader in remembering the names of the plants. In my view, what most people really want to know about wildflowers is "what is this thing?" and "tell me something interesting about it." Botanical detail, while interesting and enlightening to some of us, will turn off many people.

The plants depicted in the book are arranged first by colour and then by family. This is a logical arrangement for the non-botanist because the first thing a person notes about a flower is its colour. All of the plants shown in the book are identified by their prevailing common names. Where I knew of other common names applied to any plant, I've noted them. I have also included the scientific names of the plants. This inclusion is made to promote specificity. Common names vary significantly from one geographic area to another; scientific names do not. If you want to learn the scientific names of the plants to promote precision, that's fine. If not, no worries, but just be mindful that many plants have different common names applied to them depending on geography and local usage.

A few cautionary comments and suggestions:

While you are outdoors, go carefully among the plants so as not to damage or disturb them. Stay on the established trails; those trails exist to allow us to view the natural environment without trampling it to death. Many environments are delicate and can be significantly damaged by indiscriminately tromping around in the flora.

Do not pick the flowers. Leave them for others to enjoy.

Do not attempt to transplant wild plants. Such attempts are most often doomed to failure.

Do not eat any plants or plant parts. Do not attempt to use any plants or plant parts for medicinal purposes. To do so presents a potentially significant health hazard. Many of the plants are poisonous – some violently so.

One final cautionary note: the pursuit of wildflowers can be addictive, though not hazardous to your health.

Neil L. Jennings
Calgary, Alberta

TERRITORIAL RANGE OF WILDFLOWERS

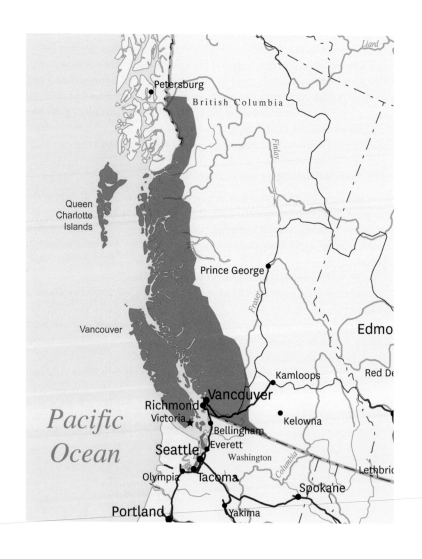

Red, Orange *and* Pink Flowers

This section contains flowers that are red, orange or pink when encountered in the field. Flowers that are pinkish can often have tones running to lavender, so if you do not find the one you are looking for here, check the other parts of the book.

Wild Ginger

Asarum canadense

BIRTHWORT FAMILY

This plant is a low, creeping, matted perennial that appears in moist, shady woods at low to mid-elevations. The paired, opposite, glossy, evergreen leaves are kidney- to heart-shaped and are borne on long, hairy stalks. The purple-brown, solitary flower nestles between the leaves, often hidden by them. The plant exudes a faint odour of ginger, and is pollinated by flies, ants, millipedes and other "creepy crawlers." Indigenous peoples used the plant for a variety of medicinal purposes. The plant is not related to the gingers used in Asian cuisine, which are in the genus *Zingiber*.

Falsebox

Paxistima myrsinites

BITTERSWEET FAMILY

This dense evergreen shrub grows at low to mid-elevations in coniferous forests. Its reddish-brown branches exhibit four ridges, and its glossy, leathery leaves are opposite and sharp-toothed. The tiny, fragrant flowers are relatively inconspicuous, being brick-red to maroon and cruciform, with four petals occurring in clusters along the branches in the leaf axils. The plant is also known as Mountain Boxwood, Oregon Boxwood and Mountain-Lover.

Water Smartweed (Water Knotweed)

Polygonum amphibium

BUCKWHEAT FAMILY

This plant occurs from prairie to subalpine elevations, and is found in ponds, marshes and ditches and along lakeshores, often forming mats in standing water. The plant may grow on land adjacent to or in the water. Its large leaves are oblong to lance-shaped, rounded or pointed at the tips, and have a prominent mid-vein. The flowers are pink and occur in a dense, oblong cluster at the top of thick, smooth stalks. The plant was used by Indigenous peoples both medicinally in poultices to treat piles and skin disease and as food. The plant is also food for a large variety of birds.

Red Columbine (Western Columbine)

Aquilegia formosa

BUTTERCUP FAMILY

These beautiful flowers are found in meadows and dry to moist woods, and are among the showiest of all western wildflowers. The leaves of the plant are mostly basal and compound, with three sets of three leaflets each. The flowers occur on stems above the basal leaves, and are composed of five yellow petal blades and five red sepals with straight spurs at their ends. The leaves on the flowering stem are considerably smaller than the basal leaves, appearing with only three leaflets each. Numerous stamens extend well beyond the petals.

Bull Thistle

Cirsium vulgare

COMPOSITE FAMILY

This Eurasian weed was introduced to North America and is now common along roadsides and in pastures, waste places and clearings. It grows to over 2 m tall and will produce a multitude of flowers. The flowers are large composite heads with purple disc flowers and no ray flowers. The flower heads are bulbous and covered in sharp spikes. The flower structure is extraordinarily intricate when examined closely. The leaves, both basal and stem, are lance-shaped, deeply lobed, spiny and clasping the stem. The species grows to heights of over 2 m and produces a multitude of flowers, which are a favourite of bees and butterflies.

Orange Agoseris (Orange-Flowered False Dandelion)

Agoseris aurantiaca

COMPOSITE FAMILY

This plant is relatively common in moist to dry openings, meadows and dry open forests in mid- to alpine elevations. Also known as False Dandelion, the plant occurs in yellow (*A. glauca*) as well as orange. Agoseris shares many characteristics with the Dandelion (*Taraxacum officinale*), but Agoseris is generally taller and its leaves are longer with the leaf blades being smooth or faintly toothed rather than deeply incised the way the Dandelion's are. Some Indigenous peoples used the milky juice of the plant as a chewing gum. Infusions from the plant were also used for a variety of medicinal purposes.

Orange Hawkweed

Hieracium aurantiacum

COMPOSITE FAMILY

Common to open woods, meadows, roadsides, ditches and disturbed areas from low to subalpine areas, this conspicuous flower was introduced from Europe, where it has long been a garden ornamental. The species can spread rapidly and become a noxious weed. The orange flower heads appear in a cluster on ascending stalks. The flowers are composed entirely of ray florets; there are no disc florets. The leaves are broadly lance- to spoon-shaped, in a basal rosette. The hawk reference in the name arises from an ancient belief that eating these plants improved a hawk's vision.

Pink Pussytoes

Antennaria rosea

COMPOSITE FAMILY

This mat-forming low perennial spreads by trailing stems, and occurs from valley floors to the subalpine zone. The spatula-shaped leaves are grey-hairy on both surfaces. The basal leaves are larger than those on the slender stem of the plant. The flower heads are composed entirely of disc florets that are pinkish in colour and surrounded by several transparently thin overlapping bracts. The name Pussytoes is a reference to the soft, fuzzy flower heads.

Flowering Red Currant (Red-Flower Currant)

Ribes sanguineum

CURRANT FAMILY

This early-blooming plant is an upright shrub that grows to 3 m tall in open, dry woods, along roadsides and in logged areas from low to mid-elevations. It has reddish-brown bark, and the leaves are triangular, deeply three-lobed, toothed and up to 6 cm wide. The numerous flowers are rose red to pink and tubular with five spreading lobes, and they occur in clusters of up to 20 flowers blooming together. The round black fruits are often covered with a blue bloom and are unpalatable.

Spreading Dogbane

Apocynum androsaemifolium

DOGBANE FAMILY

This relatively common shrub occurs in thickets and wooded areas, and has freely branching, slender stems. The egg-shaped leaves are opposite and have sharp-pointed tips. The small, pinkish, bell-shaped flowers droop from the ends of the leafy stems, usually in clusters. The petal lobes are spreading and bent back, usually with dark-pink veins. Indigenous peoples used the tough fibres from the plant to fashion strong thread for making items like bowstrings and fishing nets. The pods of the plant are poisonous if eaten.

Fireweed (Great Willowherb)

Chamaenerion angustifolium (form. *Epilobium angustifolium*)

EVENING PRIMROSE FAMILY

This plant occurs in disturbed areas, roadsides, clearings and shaded woods from low elevations to the subalpine. It is often one of the first plants to appear after a fire. The pink, four-petalled flowers bloom in long terminal clusters. Bracts between the petals are narrow. The flowers bloom from the bottom of the cluster first, then upward on the stem. The leaves are alternate and appear whorled. Fireweed is the floral emblem of the Yukon.

River Beauty (Broad-Leaved Willowherb)

Chamaenerion latifolium (form. *Epilobium latifolium*)

EVENING PRIMROSE FAMILY

This plant grows as a pioneer, often in dense colonies, on gravelly floodplains and river bars, where its dense leaves and waving pink to purple flowers often obscure the stony ground underneath. River Beauty strongly resembles common Fireweed in appearance, but it has much shorter stems, broader leaves and larger, more brilliantly coloured flowers. The flowers bloom in a short, loose, leafy inflorescence. The leaves are bluish-green and waxy, with rounded tips. The plant is also known as Dwarf Fireweed.

Foxglove
Digitalis purpurea

FIGWORT FAMILY

This European import is an erect, unbranched biennial that grows up to 2 m tall in disturbed open ground and along roadsides. The hairy, coarse-toothed leaves are alternate, ovate and up to 40 cm long. A number of pink to purple flowers appear in a one-sided raceme along the erect stem. The individual flowers are five-lobed, with the lower three lobes fused into a longer, prominent lip, the upper two into a shorter lip. There are dark-purple spots inside the lower lip. The common name arises from an old myth that foxes used the flowers to sheath their paws to make a stealthy approach to the chicken coop.

Red Monkeyflower (Lewis's Monkeyflower)
Mimulus lewisii

FIGWORT FAMILY

This plant occurs, often in large patches, along mountain streams and in other moist areas in the subalpine and alpine zones. The clasping, conspicuously veined leaves are opposite and have irregular teeth along the margins. The showy red flowers arise from the axils of the upper leaves. The flowers are funnel-shaped with two lips, which are hairy and have yellow markings. Hummingbirds and bees are attracted to these flowers.

Red Paintbrush
Castilleja miniata
FIGWORT FAMILY

This is a plant of alpine meadows, well-drained slopes, open sub-alpine forests, moist stream banks and open foothills woods, Paintbrush is widely distributed and extremely variable in colour. Its narrow, sharp-pointed leaves are linear to lance-shaped and usually without teeth or divisions, though sometimes the upper leaves have three shallow lobes. The showy red, leafy bracts, which are actually modified leaves, resemble a brush dipped in paint, hence the common name.

Wild Bleeding Heart
Dicentra flormosa
FUMITORY FAMILY

This plant grows from spreading rhizomes in moist, shady woods, along steams and in dry open areas at low to mid-elevations, often forming clumps. It has fern-like foliage. Its pink flowers are up to 2.5 cm wide and occur in a panicle of up to 20 flowers above the leaves, on leafless flowering stalks that reach 40 cm tall. The flowers are distinctively heart-shaped, with colouring that resembles a drop of blood descending from the heart.

9

Herb Robert
Geranium robertianum
GERANIUM FAMILY

This Eurasian import is usually confined to low elevations but is very adaptable. It has decumbent to ascending stems that are branched, spreading, hairy and up to 60 cm tall. The leaves are mostly on the stem and they are pinnately divided and deeply cleft, giving them a fern-like appearance. The leaves turn brilliant red and bronze colours in the fall. The five-petalled flowers are pink to reddish-purple with white pencilling, usually occurring in pairs.

Bearberry (Kinnikinnick)
Arctostaphylos uva-ursi
HEATH FAMILY

This trailing or matted evergreen shrub grows low to the ground, and has long branches with reddish, flaky bark and shiny green, leathery leaves. The flowers are pale pink and urn-shaped, appearing in clumps at the ends of the stems. The fruits are dull-red berries. The edible berries remain on the plant through the winter. The common name, Kinnikinnick, is said to be of Algonquin origin. It means "something to smoke," a reference that some Indigenous peoples used the leaves of the plant as a tobacco.

Black Huckleberry (Thinleaf Huckleberry)

Vaccinium membranaceum

HEATH FAMILY

This erect, densely branched deciduous shrub grows up to 150 cm tall at mid- to high elevations in dry to moist coniferous forests. The leaves are lance-shaped to elliptical, with pointed tips and fine-toothed margins. The leaves turn red or purple in the fall. The creamy pink flowers are urn-shaped and nodding on slender stalks. The fruits are black to dark-purple berries 8–10 mm across. Without question the berry of this plant is among the most sought-after wild berries that grow in the region.

Bog Cranberry

Vaccinium oxycoccos (also *Oxycoccus oxycoccus*)

HEATH FAMILY

This plant is a creeping, vine-like dwarf evergreen shrub that grows up to 40 cm tall in bogs and wet sphagnum moss from low to subalpine elevations. The stems are thin, wiry and slightly hairy. The small leaves are alternate, leathery, sharp-pointed and widely spaced on the stem. The leaves are dark green on the upper surface, lighter underneath, and the margins curl under. The nodding flowers are deep pink, with four petals that curve backwards.

False Azalea (Fool's Huckleberry)

Menziesia ferruginea (also *Rhododendron menziesii*)

HEATH FAMILY

This deciduous shrub is erect and spreading, and grows up to 2 m tall in moist, wooded sites from foothills to subalpine zones. The twigs of the shrub have fine, rust-coloured, sticky glandular hairs, and give off a skunky odour when crushed. The leaves are alternate, elliptical and glandular hairy, with a prominent mid-vein. The flowers are small, pinkish to greenish-orange and urn-shaped, nodding on long, slender stalks. The fruits are dark-purplish capsules which are inedible.

Oval-Leaved Blueberry

Vaccinium ovalifolium

HEATH FAMILY

This deciduous shrub grows to over 2 m tall in moist to wet coniferous forests, clearings and bogs at low to subalpine elevations. The pale pink flowers are urn-shaped and appear singly at the leaf bases. The flowers may precede the arrival of the leaves. The berries are blue-black, dusted with a pale-bluish bloom. The berries have a pleasant flavour. The genus *Vaccinium* includes all of the wild Blueberries, Cranberries and Huckleberries.

Pine-Drops

Pterospora andromedea

HEATH FAMILY

Pine-Drops is a rare saprophyte, a plant that gets its nutrients from decaying plant or animal matter. The stalk grows to 1 m tall in deep humus of coniferous or mixed woods. The leaves are mostly basal and resemble scales. The flowers are cream-coloured to yellowish, and occur in a raceme that covers roughly the top half of the stalk. The petals are united into an urn shape, and hang downward off bent flower stalks, like small lanterns. The stalks of the plant will remain erect for a year or more after the plant dies.

Pink Rhododendron

Rhododendron macrophyllum

HEATH FAMILY

This compact, rounded evergreen shrub grows to 6 m tall in coniferous forests and open thickets at low elevations in the region. Its leathery leaves are up to 20 cm long, shiny on top, and appear in whorls around the branches. The pink flowers are five-lobed, with the petals fused, and they appear in clusters at the ends of branches. The flowers have spotting in the throat. All parts of the plant contain poisonous alkaloids that are toxic to humans and livestock.

Pink Wintergreen

Pyrola asarifolia

HEATH FAMILY

This plant is an erect perennial that inhabits moist to dry coniferous and mixed forests and riverine environments from the montane to the subalpine zone. Its waxy, pale-pink to purplish-red nodding flowers are shaped like an inverted cup or bell, and have a long, curved, projecting style. The shiny, rounded, dark-green leaves are basal in a rosette and have a leathery appearance. The name "wintergreen" refers to evergreen leaves, not the flavour that has the same name.

Pipsissewa (Prince's-Pine)

Chimaphila umbellata

HEATH FAMILY

This small evergreen shrub grows to 30 cm tall in coniferous woods. Its glossy, dark-green leaves are narrowly spoon-shaped and sawtoothed, occurring in whorls. The waxy pink flowers are saucer-shaped and nodding on an erect stem above the leaves. The fruits of the plant are dry, round, brown capsules that often overwinter on the stem. "Pipsissewa" is an adaptation of the Cree name for the plant.

Red Heather (Pink Mountain Heather)

Phyllodoce empetriformis

HEATH FAMILY

This dwarf evergreen shrub grows up to 30 cm tall, and thrives in sub-alpine and alpine meadows and on slopes near timberline. Its blunt, needle-like leaves are grooved on both sides. The red to pink, urn-shaped flowers are erect and/or nodding in clusters at the top of the stems. This plant is not a true heather, but it has been called by that name for so long that it might as well be.

Salal

Gaultheria shallon

HEATH FAMILY

This evergreen plant is a sprawling shrub that grows up to 3 m tall and forms dense, impenetrable thickets in openings and coniferous forests from the coast to low mountain elevations. Its thick, leathery leaves are sharp-toothed at the tip, generally elliptical but rounded at the base. The pink, hairy, nodding flowers are urn-shaped, 7–10 mm long and occur in clusters (racemes) at the branch tips. The fruits are edible blue-black berries. Indigenous peoples made extensive use of the fruits as food, drying them and forming them into flat cakes.

Swamp Laurel
(Western Bog Laurel)

Kalmia microphylla

HEATH FAMILY

This low-growing evergreen shrub occurs in cool bogs and along stream banks and lakeshores from low to subalpine elevations. Its leathery leaves are dark green above and greyish-white beneath, often with the margins rolled under. The flowers are pink to rose coloured, with the petals fused together to form a saucer or bowl on a reddish stalk. There are 10 purple-tipped stamens protruding from the petals. The leaves and flowers of this plant contain poisonous alkaloids that can be fatal to humans and livestock if ingested.

Orange Honeysuckle
(Western Trumpet)

Lonicera ciliosa

HONEYSUCKLE FAMILY

This is a climbing vine up to 6 m long that clambers over trees and shrubs in woodlands and forest openings from low to high elevations. Its broadly elliptical leaves are up to 10 cm long and opposite on the stem, except the uppermost pair, which are connate – fused at the bases to form a shallow cup. The vividly orange, tubular flowers are up to 4 cm long, and appear in clusters of up to 25 blooms from inside the connate leaves. Unlike many members of the genus, these flowers have no scent.

Snowberry

Symphoricarpos albus

HONEYSUCKLE FAMILY

This common deciduous shrub occurs from coast to coast in North America, and is found in well-drained, open or wooded sites from prairies to lower subalpine zones. Its pale-green leaves are opposite and elliptical to oval. The flowers are pink to white and broadly funnel-shaped, occurring in clusters at the ends of the twigs. The fruits are waxy, white, berry-like drupes that occur in clusters and often persist through the winter. It is reported that some Indigenous peoples called the berries "Ghost Berries" or "Corpse Berries" and would not touch them.

Twinflower

Linnaea borealis

HONEYSUCKLE FAMILY

This small trailing evergreen is common in coniferous forests but is easily overlooked by the casual observer. The plant sends runners creeping along the forest floor, over mosses, stumps and fallen logs. At frequent intervals the runners give rise to the distinctive Y-shaped stems 5–10 cm tall. Each fork of the stem supports at its end a pink to white, slightly flared, trumpet-like flower that hangs down like a small lantern on a tiny lamppost. The flowers have a sweet perfume that is most evident near evening.

Tiger Lily
(Columbia Lily)

Lilium columbianum

LILY FAMILY

This showy lily can have up to 30 flowers per stem. The orange to orange-yellow blossoms hang downward, with reflexed petals, and have deep-red to purplish spots near the base. These spots are most probably the source of the common name Tiger Lily. The bulbs of the plants were used as food by some Indigenous peoples. They were said to have a peppery taste and would add that flavour to other foods. Over-picking has diminished the distribution of the plant.

Hooker's Onion

Allium acuminatum

LILY FAMILY

This plant grows from an ovoid, checkerboard-patterned corm in dry, rocky areas and grasslands. The corm puts up a stout, erect, leafless flowering stem that is up to 30 cm tall. There are two or three basal leaves that are linear and almost as tall as the flowering stem, but they wither prior to blooming. The inflorescence is an open umbel of up to 20 stalked flowers, each rose-pink in colour, bell-shaped and having six distinct spreading and somewhat reflexed tepals. The common name honours Sir Joseph Dalton Hooker, the first director of Kew Gardens in London.

Nodding Onion
Allium cernuum

LILY FAMILY

This plant is a common species in the region, and is easily identified by its smooth, leafless stem and drooping or nodding pink inflorescence. There are usually 8 to 12 flowers in the nodding cluster. The stem gives off a strong oniony odour when crushed. Indigenous peoples consumed the bulbs, both raw and cooked and as flavouring for other foods, and dried them for later use.

Pink Fawn Lily (Trout Lily)
Erythronium revolutum

LILY FAMILY

This early-blooming lily favours moist open woods, forest edges and stream banks, usually in sandy humus and at lower elevations. The plant has two large, dark-green, elliptical basal leaves that are very attractively mottled with brown or white. The lovely pink flower appears at the top of a smooth, leafless stem, usually as solitary, but an individual plant may have as many as three flowers. The flowers are nodding, with six reflexed tepals that often display yellow bands at the base of the inner surface. Pink Fawn Lilies are often found in large clumps.

Hedge Nettle

Stachys cooleyae
(also S. chamissonis)

MINT FAMILY

This species inhabits wetland marshes, moist woods, stream banks and lakeshores and swampy low ground. The plant has a single, bristly stem that is square in cross-section and stands up to 120 cm tall. Its coarse-toothed, wedge- to egg-shaped leaves are 10 cm long, hairy on both surfaces and occur in opposite pairs on the stem. The red-purple, tubular flowers occur in whorled, interrupted clusters in the axils of the leaves on the upper stem.

Venus Slipper (Fairy Slipper)

Calypso bulbosa

ORCHID FAMILY

This orchid is found in moist, shaded coniferous forests. The flowers are solitary and nodding on leafless stems. The flower has pinkish to purplish sepals and mauve side petals. The lip is whitish or purplish with red to purple spots or stripes, and is hairy yellow inside. The flower is on the top of a single stalk and has a deeply wrinkled appearance. This small but extraordinarily beautiful flower blooms in the early spring, often occurring in colonies.

Spotted Coralroot (Summer Coralroot)

Corallorhiza maculata

ORCHID FAMILY

A plant of moist woods and bogs, this orchid grows from extensive coral-like rhizomes. There are no leaves, but the plant has several membranous bracts that sheath the purplish to brownish stem. A number of flowers appear on each stem, loosely arranged up the stem in a raceme. The three sepals and two upper petals are reddish purple. The lip petal is white with dark-red or purple spots and two lateral lobes. The plant lacks chlorophyll and does not produce food by photosynthesis, relying instead on parasitizing various fungi in the soil.

Striped Coralroot

Corallorhiza striata

ORCHID FAMILY

This orchid grows from extensive coral-like rhizomes, and occurs in moist woods and bogs in the montane and subalpine zones. The pink to yellowish-pink flowers have purplish stripes on the sepals, and the lowest petal forms a tongue-shaped lip. A number of flowers appear on each stem, loosely arranged up the stem in an unbranched raceme. The leaves are tubular sheaths that surround, and somewhat conceal, the base of the purplish stem. The plant depends on a complex relationship with fungi in the soil for germination and survival.

Beach Pea

Lathyrus japonicus
(also *L. maritina*)

PEA FAMILY

This species grows from a rhizome and spreads out to 150 cm, trailing and climbing over other plants on sandy beaches and coastlines around the northern hemisphere. The thick and sturdy rhizome anchors the plant firmly in place in the sand. The leaves are compound, having 6–12 elliptical, leathery leaflets on sturdy stems, with tendrils at the leaf tips. The pea-like flowers are reddish-purple to bluish and occur in a loose, stalked cluster of two to eight individual flowers. The fruits are in pods that resemble those of garden peas.

Perennial Pea

Lathyrus latifolius

PEA FAMILY

This European native was introduced as a garden ornamental and has since escaped to grow in disturbed ground, along roadsides and in other low-elevation environments. The plant grows from sprawling rhizomes and can be up to 150 cm tall. The leaves are compound and opposite, with only two elliptical leaflets, which can be up to 14 cm long. Each leaf has long, many-branched tendrils at the leaf tip that allow the plant to climb over other vegetation. The reddish-pink, pea-like flowers are 2 cm long and occur in clusters of up to 15 on upright stems.

Red Clover
Trifolium pratense

PEA FAMILY

A European species now well established in North America, this plant grows to 60 cm tall in low to mid-elevations. Its leaves are in threes, often displaying a white, crescent-shaped spot near the base. The pinkish to purple flowers are pea-like, and up to 200 of them occur in dense heads 2–3 cm in diameter at stem tops. Two leaves lie immediately below the flower head. The name "clover" is derived from the Latin *clava*, which means "club."

Scarlet Pimpernel
Anagallis arvensis

PRIMROSE FAMILY

This sprawling European import is a garden escapee with decumbent to ascending stems that might reach 40 cm long. The egg-shaped leaves appear only on the stem, and are unstalked, somewhat clasping, and opposite in pairs. The salmon-pink to red flowers are solitary on curved stalks up to 4 cm long. The flowers are 5–10 mm wide, with five lobes divided almost to the bases and fringed with fine hairs. The fruits are spherical capsules that break open for seed dispersal. The flowers close if the sun is obscured, reopening when the sun returns.

Dwarf Raspberry

Rubus arcticus

ROSE FAMILY

This plant is a low, creeping dwarf shrub that grows from a trailing rootstock that is most often found in wet meadows and around seeps in the subalpine and alpine zones. The leaves are divided into three leaflets that are round to heart-shaped and have coarse-toothed edges. The flowers are usually solitary, pink and five-petalled. The fruits are clusters of red to purple drupelets, the aggregate of which is the raspberry. The fruits are small but sweet and flavourful.

Dwarf Woodland Rose (Baldhip Rose)

Rosa gymnocarpa

ROSE FAMILY

This is a slender, straggly shrub that grows to over 1 m tall in moist to dry woods and other forested areas in the region. Its leaves are pinnately compound, with 5–9 elliptical, double-toothed leaflets 4 cm long. The plant is armed with numerous slender thorns. The flowers are the familiar pink wild roses, borne singly on short stems from the leaf axils, with golden stamens in the centre of spreading pink petals. The fruits are round, shiny-red rosehips. The specific epithet, *gymnocarpa*, means "naked fruit," a reference to the fact that the rosehips do not have withered sepals attached to the fruits. This is the only member of this genus that does not retain its withered sepals.

Hardhack
(Douglas Spirea)

Spiraea douglasii

ROSE FAMILY

This erect, deciduous, freely branching shrub forms dense, impenetrable thickets up to 2 m tall in marshy areas and along streams at low to mid-elevations. Its oblong, elliptical leaves are 3–9 cm long and notched at the tips. The inflorescence is a tall, elongated cluster of hundreds of tiny pink flowers. The flowers are relatively short-lived, quickly turning brown and drab in appearance.

The common name, Hardhack, is said to have arisen because the dense thickets of the plant are hard to hack through.

Nootka Rose

Rosa nutkana

ROSE FAMILY

This medium-sized shrub grows up to 3 m tall in open habitats at low to mid-elevations. The plant is armed with a pair of large prickles near the bases of the leaves. The leaves are alternate, deciduous and pinnately compound, with five to seven egg-shaped to elliptical, saw-toothed leaflets with rounded tips. The flowers are large, as is typical of wild roses, and usually occur singly at the ends of branches. The fruits are round, purplish-red rosehips that have the withered sepals attached as a beard.

Salmonberry

Rubus spectabilis

ROSE FAMILY

This perennial, early blooming bush grows up to 4 m tall from rhizomes in moist woods and along streams at low to montane elevations. Its arching stems have shredding bark and are armed with numerous short, straight prickles. The leaves are trifoliate, with pointed leaflets and coarsely double-toothed margins. The flowers are showy, with five reddish-pink spreading petals, and occur singly or in small groups at the ends of the stems. The large red fruit is a sweet, soft, edible berry that is up to 2.5 cm long.

Roseroot

Rhodiola integrifolia (form. *Sedum integrifolium*)

STONECROP FAMILY

This plant occurs in the subalpine and alpine zones, favouring moist, rocky scree, talus and ridges. The stems arise from a fleshy rootstock, and they are covered in persistent leaves. The leaves are oval to oblong, fleshy and somewhat flattened. The rose-coloured to purple flowers have oblong petals and occur in dense, rounded, flat-topped clusters atop the stems. When the roots are cut or bruised, they give off the fragrance of roses, hence the common name.

White, Green *and* Brown Flowers

This section includes flowers that are predominantly white or cream-coloured, green or brown when encountered in the field. Given that some flowers fade to other colours as they age, if you do not find the one you are looking for here, check the other parts of the book.

Vanilla Leaf

Achlys triphylla

BARBERRY FAMILY

This plant spreads by rhizomes, and will carpet the understorey in shady, moist places in deep woods, open parkland and forest edges. Its large leaves are divided into three leaflets, similar to huge clover leaves, with scalloped margins that appear winged and will nod with even the slightest of breezes. The tiny white flowers appear on an erect stalk that rises above the leaves. The fruits are small, mahogany-coloured seeds that are shaped like a half moon. The leaves, when dried, emit a distinct odour of vanilla, hence the common name for the plant.

Buckbrush (Redstem Ceanothus)

Ceanothus sanguineus

BUCKTHORN FAMILY

This erect deciduous shrub grows to 3 m tall in forest openings and edges, clearings and disturbed sites in the montane and subalpine zones. Its smooth, erect stems are numerous and become purple-red with age. The egg-shaped to elliptical leaves are 10 cm long, alternate, fine-toothed, and hairy on the underside. The fragrant flowers are white, and bloom in dense, fluffy clusters on reddish stems on lateral branches from last year's growth. Deer and elk use the plant for winter browse.

Mountain Sorrel
Oxyria digyna
BUCKWHEAT FAMILY

This relatively low-growing plant often appears in clumps along streams, at lake margins and in moist rocky places in the subalpine and alpine zones. Its long-stalked, primarily basal, often reddish leaves are smooth with wavy margins and are distinctively kidney- or heart-shaped. The tiny green to reddish flowers appear in crowded clusters along several upright stems and are relatively inconspicuous. The fruits are flat, red, papery seeds that have broad translucent wings. Mammals and birds eat this species, and a number of Indigenous peoples also used it as a food.

Sulphur Buckwheat
Eriogonum umbellatum
BUCKWHEAT FAMILY

This perennial grows from a stout taproot and tends to be mat forming. Its spoon- to egg-shaped leaves are all basal, narrowing to a slender stalk, greenish above and often woolly white beneath. The leaves turn bright red in the fall. The flowering stem is usually leafless and up to 30 cm tall. The stem supports an inflorescence composed of small creamy-white to pale-yellow flowers that are held in compact spherical clusters (umbels). The flowers sometimes become tinged with pink on aging. The plant occurs from moderate to alpine elevations on grassy slopes, dry gravel ridges, alpine ridges and talus slopes.

The specific epithet, *umbellatum*, refers to the shape of the inflorescence, and indeed the species also goes by the locally common name Subalpine Umbrellaplant.

Lyall's Anemone (Western Wood Anemone)

Anemone lyallii

BUTTERCUP FAMILY

This plant grows in moist forests and openings from low to subalpine elevations. The stem is erect with three distinctive compound leaves whorled at mid-stem. The leaves are on long stems (petioles) and are divided into three-lobed leaflets that have coarse, rounded teeth. The small flowers are white to pink to pale blue and have only sepals, no petals. *Anemone* is said to derive from the Greek *anemo*, meaning "wind," a reference to the fact that the seeds of members of the genus are distributed by the wind.

Baneberry

Actaea rubra

BUTTERCUP FAMILY

This perennial grows up to 1 m tall in moist, shady woods and thickets, along streams and in clearings from low to subalpine elevations. It has one to several stout, upright, branching stems. Its coarse-toothed leaves are all on the stem and are divided two or three times into threes. The inflorescence is a dense, white, cone-shaped cluster of flowers that appears on top of a spike. The fruit is a large cluster of either shiny red or white berries. The leaves, roots and berries of this plant are extremely poisonous.

False Bugbane (Carolina Bugbane)

Trautvetteria caroliniensis

BUTTERCUP FAMILY

This attractive and distinctive perennial grows from a rhizome along stream banks and in moist woods. The leaves are mostly basal, toothed, wider than long and deeply palmately lobed. The flowers are borne at the terminal ends of an erect, branched stalk that might be as much as 80 cm tall. The white flowers have no petals, only white sepals and many stamens, giving the flower heads the look of round powder puffs.

Globeflower

Trollius albiflorus

BUTTERCUP FAMILY

This plant grows from thick rootstock and fibrous roots, and is found in moist meadows, along stream banks and in open, damp areas in the subalpine and alpine zones. Its shiny, bright-green, mostly basal leaves are palmately divided into five to seven parts and deeply toothed. The stem leaves are few, alternate and short-stalked. The flowers are made up of five to ten white sepals (which may have a pinkish tint on the outside) that surround a central core filled with numerous dark-yellow stamens. This plant contains a poisonous alkaloid.

Mountain Marsh Marigold

Caltha leptosepala

BUTTERCUP FAMILY

This plant lives along stream banks and in marshes and seeps in the subalpine and alpine zones. Its simple, long-stemmed, mostly basal leaves are oblong to bluntly arrowhead-shaped, with wavy or round-toothed margins. The flowers are solitary on the end of the stem, and consist of up to a dozen white, petal-like sepals that are tinged with blue on the back. The flower has a bright-yellow centre composed of numerous stamens and pistils. This plant contains glucosides which are poisonous.

Western Anemone (Chalice Flower)

Pulsatilla occidentalis (also *Anemone occidentalis*)

BUTTERCUP FAMILY

This plant is considered by many to be emblematic of wet alpine meadows and clearings. Its large, creamy-white flowers bloom early in the spring as the leaves are beginning to emerge. The entire plant is covered with hairs, which keep it protected in its cold habitat. Most of the leaves are basal, but there is a ring of feathery, grey-green stem leaves just below the flower. The flower is replaced by a clump of plumed seeds at the tip of the flowering stem. Some people refer to this stage as "Hippies on a Stick."

Chocolate Tips (Fern-Leaved Desert Parsley)

Lomatium dissectum

CARROT FAMILY

This large plant has several stout, smooth, hairless stems, and grows to over 1 m tall in dry, rocky places. Its large, finely dissected leaves are fern-like and have a spicy aroma. The surface of the leaves has a covering of fine hairs, making it rough to the touch. The flowers are compound umbels of deep-purplish-brown or yellow flowers sitting atop the ends of the stems. The fruits are elliptical seeds with flattened backs and corky, thick-winged margins.

Cow Parsnip

Heracleum lanatum

CARROT FAMILY

A denizen of shaded riverine habitat, stream banks, seeps and moist open woods, this plant grows to over 2 m tall. The flowers are distinctive in large, compound, umbrella-shaped clusters (umbels) composed of numerous white flowers, with white petals in fives. The leaves, compound in threes, are usually very large, softly hairy, toothed and deeply lobed.

Queen Anne's Lace

Daucus carota

CARROT FAMILY

This is an invasive weed imported from Eurasia that is now common in disturbed ground, moist meadows, fields and roadsides all over North America. It is a single-stemmed biennial that grows to 120 cm tall. The leaves are very finely dissected, like those of garden carrot plants. The inflorescence occurs as compound umbels in compact heads of hundreds of tiny yellow-white flowers atop the stem. The central floret in the umbel is often purple or pink. When the plant goes to seed, the outer, longer spokes of the umbel arch inwards, forming a "bird's nest" effect.

Water Hemlock

Cicuta maculata
(also *C. douglasii*)

CARROT FAMILY

This is a plant of marshes, river and stream banks, and low, wet areas. It produces several large umbrella-like clusters (compound umbels) of white flowers appearing at the top of a sturdy stalk. The leaves are alternate and twice compound, with many lance-shaped leaflets. The primary lateral veins in the leaves end between the notched teeth on the leaflets rather than at their points. This is unique, and separates this species from parsley family members in the area.

While lovely to look at, the Water Hemlock is considered to be perhaps the most poisonous plant in North America. All parts of the plant are toxic, as testified to by several of its common names, including Children's Bane, Beaver Poison and Death Of Man.

Daisy Fleabane (Cut-Leaf Daisy)

Erigeron compositus

COMPOSITE FAMILY

The leaves of this species are almost all basal and are deeply divided. The leaves and flowering stems are sparsely covered with short, glandular hairs. The flowers appear solitary at the top of the stem, and are composed of ray flowers surrounding disc flowers. The ray flowers are numerous and may be white, pink or mauve in colour. The disc flowers are numerous and yellow. The common name Fleabane arose because it was once thought that bundles of these flowers brought into the house would repel fleas.

Ox-Eye Daisy

Leucanthemum vulgare

COMPOSITE FAMILY

This invasive Eurasian perennial grows from a well developed rhizome at low to mid- elevations in moist to moderately dry sites such as roadsides, clearings, pastures and disturbed areas. Its flowers are solitary composite heads at the ends of branches, and include white ray flowers and yellow disc flowers. The basal leaves are broadly lance-shaped or narrowly spoon-shaped. The stem leaves are oblong and smaller. This species is very prolific and will overgrow large areas if not kept in check. Many people consider it the most common and recognizable wildflower in North America.

Pathfinder Plant (Trail Plant)

Adenocaulon bicolor

COMPOSITE FAMILY

This species grows in shady and open woods at low to moderate elevations. Its somewhat large basal leaves are triangular, alternate and narrowly scalloped, and can reach 1 m long. The leaves are green above and white woolly beneath. The flowering stem is solitary with many branches, rising above the leaves, and has inconspicuous white flowers at the top. The fruits are hooked achenes that cling to clothing or fur of passersby. The common name arises because the leaves invert when a hiker passes through, leaving a trail of silvery-white undersides apparent.

Pearly Everlasting

Anaphalis margaritacea

COMPOSITE FAMILY

This plant grows in gravelly open woods and subalpine meadows in the mountains. It has numerous stem leaves, alternately attached directly to the stem. The leaves are light green and lance-shaped with very soft, fuzzy hairs. The white flowers occur in a dense, rounded terminal cluster. The male and female flowers occur on separate plants. The flowers have only disc flowers, no ray flowers, and often have a brown spot at the base. As the common name might suggest, the flowers persist for a long time.

Bunchberry (Dwarf Dogwood)

Cornus canadensis

DOGWOOD FAMILY

This is a plant of moist coniferous woods, often found on rotting logs and stumps. The flowers are clusters of inconspicuous greenish-white flowers set among four white, showy, petal-like bracts. The leaves are in a terminal whorl of four to seven, all prominently veined, and are dark-green above, lighter underneath. The fruits are bright-red berries. The plant's common name, Bunchberry, is probably derived from the fact that the fruits are all bunched together in a terminal cluster when ripe.

Pacific Dogwood (Western Flowering Dogwood)

Cornus nuttallii

DOGWOOD FAMILY

This irregularly branched deciduous tree reaches heights of up to 20 m. Its bark is smooth and blackish-brown, becoming ridged with age. Its opposite, oval, stalked leaves are pointed at the ends, with distinctive paired veins that curve parallel to the leaf margins. The leaves turn to gorgeous reds in the autumn. The tree flowers in the spring with tremendous numbers of large, cream-coloured blossoms. The flowers individually are small, greenish white, numerous and inconspicuous, occurring in spherical clusters that are surrounded by four to seven very conspicuous white (sometimes pink-fringed), petal-like showy bracts.

Sickletop Lousewort (Parrot's Beak)

Pedicularis racemosa

FIGWORT FAMILY

This lovely plant favours upper montane and subalpine environments. Its white flower has a very distinctive shape that deserves close examination to appreciate its intricacy. It is variously described as similar to a sickle, a tool with a short handle and a curved blade, or as resembling a parrot's beak, thus explaining the most-often used common names. The flowers appear along a purplish stem that grows up to 35 cm tall. The simple leaves are lance-shaped to linear and have distinctive fine, sharp teeth on the margins. Another locally common name for this plant is Leafy Lousewort

Greenish-Flowered Wintergreen (Green Wintergreen)

Pyrola chlorantha

HEATH FAMILY

This is an erect perennial that inhabits riverine environments and moist to dry coniferous and mixed forests from montane to subalpine zones. Its flowers have five waxy, greenish-white petals and a long style attached to a prominent ovary. The bell-shaped flowers are distributed on short stalks up the main stem. The shiny, rounded, dark-green leaves are evergreen, basal in a rosette and have a leathery appearance.

One-Sided Wintergreen

Pyrola secunda
(also *Orthilia secunda*)

HEATH FAMILY

This small forest dweller grows up to 15 cm tall at low to subalpine elevations in dry to moist coniferous or mixed woods and clearings. The white to yellowish-green flowers lie on one side of the arching stalk, arranged in a raceme of six to ten and sometimes more. The flowers resemble small street lights strung along a curving pole. The straight style sticks out beyond the petals, with a flat, five-lobed stigma. The egg-shaped, evergreen leaves are basal and fine-toothed at their margins. Once seen, this lovely little flower is unmistakable in the woods.

Single Delight (One-Flowered Wintergreen)

Moneses uniflora

HEATH FAMILY

This intriguing little forest dweller inhabits damp forests, usually on rotting wood. The plant is quite tiny, standing only 15 cm tall, and its single white flower, open and nodding at the top of the stem, is less than 5 cm in diameter. The flower looks like a small white umbrella offering shade. The leaves are basal, oval and evergreen, attached to the base of the stem. The style is prominent and tipped with a five-lobed stigma that almost looks like a mechanical part of some kind. The plant is also known locally as Wood Nymph and Shy Maiden.

White Rhododendron

Rhododendron albiflorum

HEATH FAMILY

This is an erect and spreading deciduous shrub that grows up to 2 m tall in cool, damp woods, often establishing dense communities under the conifer canopy. The leaves are oblong to lance-shaped and covered with fine rust-coloured hairs. The large white, cup-shaped flowers are borne singly or in small clusters around the stem. They are also deciduous and fall from the plant intact, often littering the forest floor with what appear to be whole flowers. All parts of the plant contain poisonous alkaloids.

Red Twinberry (Utah Honeysuckle)

Lonicera utahensis

HONEYSUCKLE FAMILY

This erect deciduous shrub grows up to 2 m tall at low to subalpine elevations in moist to wet forest openings and clearings in the southern portion of the region. The leaves are opposite and elliptical to oblong with smooth edges and blunt tips. The creamy-white flowers are trumpet-shaped and appear in pairs on a single stalk from the leaf axils. The fruits are red berries that are joined at the base. Some Indigenous peoples ate the berries, which were said to be a good emergency source of water because they are so juicy.

Mock Orange

Philadelphus lewisii

HYDRANGEA FAMILY

This erect deciduous shrub is stiffly and densely branched, growing up to 3 m tall in thickets and crevices, on rocky hillsides and along streams from valley to subalpine elevations. Its leaves occur in opposite pairs on the stems, and the bark of the shrub is reddish-brown to grey. The plant flowers in the late spring, producing lots of white flowers that have four oblong white petals, four styles and many stamens. The flower emits a sweet orange-blossom aroma. The fruits are hard capsules that overwinter on the shrub.

Bronzebells

Stenanthium occidentale

LILY FAMILY

This lily of moist woods, stream banks, meadows and slopes has grass-like leaves that emerge from an onion-like bulb. The bell-shaped flowers are greenish-white flecked with purple, and have six sharp-pointed tips that twist backward, exposing the interior of the blossom. Ten or more graceful and fragrant flowers hang along the length of the stem, drooping down. Some authorities say this plant is poisonous, others say it is not.

Clasping-Leaved Twisted-Stalk

Streptopus amplexifolius

LILY FAMILY

This is a plant of moist, shaded forests. It has a widely branching, zigzag stem with numerous sharp-pointed, parallel-veined leaves that encircle the stem at each bend. The glossy leaves often conceal the small, pale-white or greenish flowers that dangle on curving, threadlike stalks from the axil of each upper leaf. In fact, one could walk right past this plant without even noticing its flowers, which appear to be hanging like small spiders dangling on fine webs. The fruits of this species are very handsome orangish-red oval berries.

Fairybells

Prosartes hookeri
(form. *Disporum hookeri*)

LILY FAMILY

A plant of moist, shaded woods, stream banks and riverine environments, this delightful flower blooms in early summer. Its creamy-white, bell-shaped flowers have six tepals and occur in drooping pairs at the end of branches. The leaves of the plant are generally lance-shaped, with parallel veins and pointed ends. The fruits are reddish-orange, egg-shaped berries occurring in pairs. The fruits of the plant are edible, but said to be bland. They are a favoured food of many rodents and birds.

Queen's Cup

Clintonia uniflora

LILY FAMILY

This beautiful perennial lily grows from slender rhizomes. The flowers are about 5 cm in diameter, and are usually solitary, white and cup-shaped, appearing at the top of an erect, hairy stem. The plant may display two or three shiny leaves at the base of its flowering stem, each of them oblong or elliptical, with hairy edges. Its fruit is a single deep-blue berry, giving rise to two locally common names: Beadlily and Bluebead Lily.

Star-Flowered Solomon's-Seal

Maianthemum stellatum

LILY FAMILY

This is a lily of moist woods, river and stream banks, thickets and meadows at montane to sub-alpine elevations. Its white star-shaped flowers are arrayed in a loose, short-stalked cluster, often on a zigzag stem. The numerous, alternate leaves are broadly lance-shaped, gradually tapering to a pointed tip, with prominent parallel veining, sometimes folded at the midline. The fruit is a cluster of green to cream-coloured berries with maroon to brown stripes.

Western Trillium (Western Wake Robin)

Trillium ovatum

LILY FAMILY

This gorgeous lily blooms early and prefers boggy, rich soils in montane and lower subalpine forests. Its large, distinctive, stalkless leaves are broadly egg-shaped with sharp tips, and occur in a whorl of three below the flower. The solitary flower blooms atop a short stem above the leaves, with three broad white petals up to 5 cm long alternating with three narrow green sepals. The petals change colour with age, first turning pink, then progressing to purple.

White Fawn Lily (Trout Lily)

Erythronium oregonum

LILY FAMILY

This early blooming lily favours moist open woods, forest edges and stream banks, usually in sandy humus at lower elevations. The plant has two large, dark-green, elliptical, basal leaves that are very attractively mottled with brown or white. The lovely white flower appears at the top of a smooth leafless stem, usually as solitary, but an individual plant may have as many as three flowers. The flowers are nodding, with six reflexed tepals that often display yellow bands at the base of their inner surfaces. These plants are often found in large clumps.

Morning Glory (Hedge Bindweed)

Calystegia sepium (also *Convolvulus sepium*)

MORNING GLORY FAMILY

This plant is a twining, climbing or trailing vine that grows from slender, spreading rhizomes. Its white to pinkish flowers are 3–6 cm across and trumpet- or funnel-shaped. The leaves are alternate and arrowhead-shaped, and the flowers appear solitary in the leaf axils. The flowers usually close when it is dark, overcast or raining. Other locally common names for the plant are Lady's Nightcap and Bell-Bind.

Alaska Rein Orchid

Piperia unalascensis

ORCHID FAMILY

This orchid grows up to 90 cm tall from an egg-shaped tuber at low to mid-elevations in dry to moist forests and on dry, rocky open slopes. The plant has two to five lance-shaped basal leaves up to 15 cm long and 4 cm wide which usually wither before the flowers bloom. The inflorescence is a spirally arranged, spike-like raceme at the top of the stem. The small greenish to white flowers are moderately fragrant, and have a triangular lip with a spur of about equal size.

Heart-Leaved Twayblade

Listera cordata

ORCHID FAMILY

This small orchid, standing about 20 cm tall, prefers a cool, damp, mossy habitat. As a consequence of its size and preferred location, it is an easy flower to miss. Its white flowers are scattered up the stem in an open raceme. The lip of the flower is deeply split, almost in two. The stem leaf structure of the genus is distinctive, with two leaves appearing opposite each other partway up the stem. The specific epithet, *cordata*, means "heart-shaped," a reference to the leaves.

Hooded Ladies' Tresses

Spiranthes romanzoffiana

ORCHID FAMILY

This orchid is reasonably common in swampy places, along lakeshores and in meadows and open, shady woods. It grows up to 60 cm tall. The characteristic feature of the plant is its crowded flower spike, which can contain up to 60 densely spaced white flowers that appear to coil around the end of the stem in three spiralling ranks. When newly bloomed, the flower has a wonderful aroma which most people say smells like vanilla. The common name is a reference to the braid-like appearance of the flowers, similar to a braid in a lady's hair.

Mountain Lady's Slipper
Cypripedium montanum

ORCHID FAMILY

This distinctive and relatively rare orchid grows up to 60 cm tall, occurring in dry to moist woods and open areas from mid- to subalpine elevations. Its lower petal forms a white, pouch-shaped lower lip that has purple markings. The brownish sepals and lateral petals have wavy margins and appear to spiral away from the stem. The attractive leaves are alternate, broadly elliptical and clasping on the stem, and have prominent veins. One to three flowers can appear on the stem, and they are wonderfully fragrant.

Western Rattlesnake Plantain
Goodyera oblongifolia

ORCHID FAMILY

This orchid occurs in shaded, dry or moist coniferous woods in the mountains. It is a single-stemmed, stiff-hairy perennial that grows up to 40 cm tall. The basal leaves are distinctive, with a white-mottled mid-vein and whitish lateral veins. The robust downy spike bears small, greenish-white flowers in a loose, one-sided or twisted raceme, with the lower flowers blooming first. The lip of the flower has a wide-open mouth, pressed up against the overhanging hood.

White Clover (Dutch Clover)

Trifolium repens

PEA FAMILY

This common plant was introduced from Eurasia for hay, pasture and soil improvement because it is a nitrogen fixer. The leaves, which creep along the ground, are composed of three leaflets – occasionally four if you are lucky. The flowers are white and clustered on short, slender stalks in round heads. On close examination the flower cluster is quite intricate in shape and worthy of close examination. Historically the flowers have been used to flavour cheese and tobacco, and have even been used in famine times to make bread.

Mouse-Ear Chickweed (Field Chickweed)

Cerastium arvense

PINK FAMILY

This early-blooming plant thrives in dry grasslands and rocky and disturbed ground, often forming large mats of white flowers in the spring. The flowers appear in loose clusters, often numerous on each plant. The five white petals are notched and have green lines on them as nectar guides for insects. The upper part of the leaf is said to resemble a mouse's ear, thus the common name for the plant.

Sweet-Flowered Androsace (Rock Jasmine)

Androsace chamaejasme

PRIMROSE FAMILY

This striking, low-growing cushion plant is seldom more than 10 cm tall, but it can form mats of flowers on rocky ledges and in fields. The flowers are borne on a single white-hairy stem, and they occur in umbels of four or five flowers. The petals of the flowers are white, with a yellow or orange eye. Though small, these flowers have a wonderful aroma that is worth getting down on hands and knees to experience.

Western Spring Beauty

Claytonia lanceolata

PURSLANE FAMILY

The flowers of this early bloomer are white but may appear pink owing to the reddish veins in the petals and to the pink anthers. The tips of the petals are distinctly notched. The plants are usually less than 20 cm tall, and the flowers appear in loose, short-stalked terminal clusters. The species grows from a small, white, edible corm. Some Indigenous peoples used the corm as food, and it is said to taste similar to a potato.

Indian Plum (Osoberry)

Oemleria cerasiformis

ROSE FAMILY

This erect, loosely branched deciduous shrub grows up to 4 m tall in dry to moist open woods and along stream banks at low elevations. Its fuzzy, lance-shaped leaves, up to 12 cm long, are green above and grey-green beneath. The flowers appear from the leaf axils early in the spring in drooping racemes of bell-shaped white flowers. The flowers precede or coincide with the emergence of the leaves. The fruits are drupes borne on red stems. They are orange when young, blue-black at maturity.

Ocean Spray (Cream Bush)

Holodiscus discolor

ROSE FAMILY

This deciduous shrub is erect and loosely branched, growing to more than 3 m tall on coastal bluffs and in dry to moist woods. Its ovate leaves, toothed and lobed, are up to 8 cm long and woolly hairy underneath. The flowers are large pyramidal clusters of tiny white flowers that occur at the branch ends. The species is aptly named, as its clusters of white flowers bring to mind the foam cast about by crashing waves and ocean winds. The plant has a sweet scent from a distance, but is said to be musty smelling in close proximity.

Pacific Ninebark

Physocarpus capitatus

ROSE FAMILY

This is an erect to spreading deciduous shrub that grows to 4 m tall in streamside thickets, moist woods and along lake margins at low to middle elevations. Its bark is brown and shredding. The alternate, toothed leaves are dark-green above, lighter beneath, with three to five lobes and conspicuous veining. The flowers are small and white, with five petals and numerous stamens, and they occur in rounded clusters at the ends of the branches. The fruits are reddish bunches of dried, inflated follicles.

Partridgefoot (Creeping Spiraea)

Luetkea pectinata

ROSE FAMILY

This dwarf evergreen shrub creates extensive mats as it creeps over the ground on scree slopes and in moist meadows and shady areas near timberline. It often grows where snow melts late in the season. Its numerous, mainly basal leaves are smooth, fan-shaped and much divided. Old leaves wither and persist for long periods of time. The white to cream-coloured flowers appear in short, crowded clusters atop erect stems. The flowers have four to six pistils and about 20 stamens, which are conspicuous on the flowers.

Western Mountain Ash

Sorbus scopulina

ROSE FAMILY

This erect to spreading deciduous shrub grows to 4 m tall in moist open or shaded places from foothills to subalpine zones. The branches are slightly white-hairy and sticky when new, reddish-grey to yellowish when mature. The leaves are alternate and pinnately compound, with 11–13 leaflets per leaf. The white, saucer-shaped flowers have five broad petals and occur in large flat-topped clusters. The glossy orange to red fruits are berry-like pomes in dense clusters.

White Dryad (White Mountain Avens)

Dryas octopetala

ROSE FAMILY

This dwarf evergreen grows close to the ground, forming mats on gravelly soil in the alpine zone. Its leathery, dark green leaves are oblong to lance-shaped, with edges that are scalloped and often rolled under. The cream-coloured flowers bloom in abundance soon after snows melt. The flowers are borne on short, hairy, leafless stems that rise from the mats of leaves. Each flower has eight petals, thus the species name *octopetala*.

Bishop's Cap (Bare-stemmed Mitrewort)

Mitella nuda

SAXIFRAGE FAMILY

This wonderful species occurs along streams and in bogs, thickets and moist to dry forests from the montane to the subalpine. The plant stands erect and grows up to 20 cm tall. Its heart- to kidney-shaped leaves are basal and short-lobed, with rounded teeth. The tiny flowers occur in an open cluster scattered up the leafless stem. The saucer-shaped flowers are very distinctive, and when examined closely they are reminiscent of some kind of satellite dish such as might be found in outer space, complete with antennae festooned around the circumference of the flower.

Foamflower (False Mitrewort)

Tiarella trifoliate var. *laciniata*

SAXIFRAGE FAMILY

These beautiful flowers inhabit moist coniferous woods, stream banks and trails from low to subalpine elevations. The plant grows up to 50 cm tall, and the flowers are white or pinkish, arranged in open panicles well above the leaves. The leaves are compound, usually with three leaflets. The middle leaflet is usually three-lobed and toothed.

Leather-Leaved Saxifrage

Leptarrhena pyrolifolia

SAXIFRAGE FAMILY

This plant occurs in wet open forests and meadows, along streams and in seeps in the subalpine and alpine zones. Its leathery, oval to oblong, mostly basal leaves are prominently veined and have toothed edges. The purplish stems are erect, up to 40 cm tall, and have only one to three small leaves. The flowers are small and white, sometimes pink, and appear in tight clusters at the top of the flowering stem. The fruits of the plant are perhaps more striking than the flowers. The paired, pointed fruits are purplish-red, single-chambered capsules in clusters atop the stem.

Spotted Saxifrage
Saxifraga bronchialis

SAXIFRAGE FAMILY

These beautiful flowers inhabit rocky crevices, rock faces, screes and open slopes, often appearing as if by magic from the rocks. The white flowers appear in clusters at the top of the wiry brown stems, and have small red or yellow spots near the tips of the five petals. A close examination of this beautiful flower is well worth the time.

Roundleaf Sundew
Drosera rotundifolia

SUNDEW FAMILY

This odd little plant lives in bogs, swamps and fens, where it often forms colonies. It stands up to 25 cm tall and is insectivorous, meaning it eats insects, which are usually in no short supply in this species' preferred habitat. Its basal leaves are erect to ascending, with round blades on stalks up to 9 cm long, and have long reddish hairs along their margins, each hair tipped with a sticky, insect-trapping fluid. The small white flowers occur on only one side, at the top of a naked flowering stem. The flowers open only in full sun.

Blue *and* Purple Flowers

This section includes flowers that are predominantly blue or purple when encountered in the field, ranging from pale blue to deep purple, light violet to lavender. Some of the lighter hues of blue and purple might shade into pinks, so if you do not find the flower your are looking for here, check the other parts of the book.

Common Butterwort

Pinguicula vulgaris

BLADDERWORT FAMILY

This small plant is one of only a few carnivorous ones in the region. It grows from fibrous roots in bogs, seeps and wetlands and along stream banks and lakeshores from valleys to the subalpine zone. Its pale-green to yellowish leaves are basal, short-stalked, somewhat overlapping and curled in at the margins, forming a rosette on the ground. The leaves have glandular hairs on their upper surface that exude a sticky substance that attracts and then ensnares small insects. The flower is pale to dark purple and solitary atop a leafless stem.

Forget-Me-Not

Myosotis laxa

BORAGE FAMILY

This beautiful little flower is easily recognized by its wheel-shaped blue corolla and its prominent yellow eye. The stems are hairy and slender, and weak enough for the plant to often be decumbent (lying on the ground). The lower leaves are oblong to lance-shaped, while the middle to upper ones are more elliptical. The flowers appear in clusters at the top of flowering stems. The blue petals are fused at the base into a tube that spreads flat at the top. This plant occurs at lower elevations in moist habitats.

Menzies Larkspur

Delphinium menziesii

BUTTERCUP FAMILY

This is the most common of the coastal Larkspurs, appearing in grassy meadows and on rocky bluffs. It is an upright, hairy stemmed perennial that grows to 60 cm tall. Its leaves are round and deeply dissected two or three times. The distinctive flowers are highly modified, with the upper sepal forming a large, hollow, nectar-producing spur. The sepals are deep blue to purple. The petals are veined and have wavy margins. The upper two petals are often white. The flowers bloom up the stem in a loose, elongated cluster.

Monkshood

Aconitum columbianum

BUTTERCUP FAMILY

A plant of moist mixed coniferous forests and meadows, Monkshood has a distinctive flower construction that is unmistakable. The dark-blue to purple flowers appear in terminal open clusters, and the sepals form a hood like those worn by monks. The long-stalked leaves are alternate and shaped like large maple leaves. The plant contains poisonous alkaloids that can cause death within a few hours.

Blue Sailors (Chicory)

Cichorium intybus

COMPOSITE FAMILY

This native of Eurasia grows up to 1.75 m tall at low elevations on dry plateaus and in fields, grasslands and waste areas. Its basal leaves are lance-shaped and strongly toothed to lobed. The flowers have sky-blue ray flowers and no disc flowers, and they occur singly or in small groups widely spaced on the long branches. The flowers open only in the daylight. The stems exude a bitter-tasting, milky juice when broken.

Oyster Plant (Purple Salsify)

Tragopogon porrifolius

COMPOSITE FAMILY

An inhabitant of grasslands, roadsides, ditches and dry waste areas, Oyster Plant, also known as Purple Salsify, was introduced from Europe. The flower is a large, erect, solitary purple head surrounded by long, narrow, protruding green bracts. The leaves are alternate, fleshy and narrow but broad and clasping at the base. The fruit is a mass of narrow, ribbed, beaked white achenes that resembles the seed pod of a common dandelion but is significantly larger, approaching the size of a softball.

Tall Purple Fleabane

Erigeron peregrinus

COMPOSITE FAMILY

This plant grows up to 70 cm tall from a thick rootstock in the subalpine and alpine zones. Its basal leaves are narrow and stemmed, while the stem leaves are smaller and stalkless. The flowers resemble daisies, with 30–80 rose- to purple-coloured ray florets surrounding a yellow centre of disc florets. The large flowers are usually solitary, but there may be smaller ones that appear from the axils of the upper leaves.

Alpine Speedwell (Alpine Veronica)

Veronica wormskjoldii
(also *V. alpina*)

FIGWORT FAMILY

This erect perennial stands up to 30 cm tall, and is found in moist meadows and along streams in the subalpine and alpine zones. Its leaves are elliptical to egg-shaped, and occur in opposite pairs spaced along the stem. The stems, leaves and stalks of the flowers are covered with fine, sticky hairs. The flowers are numerous and occur at the top of the stem. The corolla has four united blue petals, which exhibit dark veins.

Slender Speedwell
Veronica filiformis

FIGWORT FAMILY

This Eurasian import is a very invasive, prostrate, mat-forming species. It spreads by vegetative propagation rather than seed. If parts of the plant are chopped to bits, as by mowing, the scattered pieces will take root. The small, solitary, light-blue flowers are borne on thread-like stems that arise from the leaf axils. The flowers have four somewhat asymmetrical, spreading lobes, with two stamens and a single pistil that is clubbed at the top.

Small-Flowered Blue-Eyed Mary
Collinsia parviflora

FIGWORT FAMILY

This small, early blooming annual grows on open slopes and mossy outcrops and in grassy areas from lower to middle elevations. The plant has single or branched stems that are slender and weak, causing the plant to sprawl. The leaves are opposite, narrowly egg-shaped to linear, and tapered to the base and tip. The upper leaves often appear in whorls of three to five leaflets. The small, two-lipped flowers are pale-blue and white on the upper lip, blue on the lower, and emerge from the axils of the upper leaves. The upper lip has two lobes, while the lower one has three, with the middle one folded inwards.

Small-Flowered Penstemon (Slender Beardtongue)

Penstemon procerus

FIGWORT FAMILY

This plant grows up to 40 cm tall at low to alpine elevations, usually in dry to moist open forests, grassy clearings, meadows and disturbed areas. Most of the blunt to lance-shaped leaves appear in opposite pairs up the stem. The small blue to purple flowers are funnel-shaped and appear in one to several tight clusters arranged in whorls around the stem and at its tip. The common name, Beardtongue, describes the hairy, tongue-like staminode in the throat of the flower.

Northern Gentian

Gentianella amarella
(also *Gentiana amarella*)

GENTIAN FAMILY

This plant is found in moist places in meadows, woods and ditches and along stream banks up to the subalpine zone. The flowers are first sighted by their star-like formation winking at the top of the corolla tube, amidst adjacent grasses. The plant is most often small, standing only 15–20 cm tall. The flowers appear in clusters in the axils of the upper stem leaves, the leaves being opposite and appearing almost to be small hands holding up the flowers for inspection. There is a fringe inside the throat of the flower.

Harebell

Campanula rotundifolia

HAREBELL FAMILY

This plant is widespread in a variety of habitats, including grasslands, gullies, moist forests, clearings and rocky open ground. The bell-shaped flowers are purplish-blue with hairless sepals, nodding on a thin stem in loose clusters. The leaves are lance-shaped and thin on the stem. The heart-shaped basal leaves are coarse-toothed and usually wither before the flowers appear. *Campanula* is Latin meaning "little bell."

Narrow-Leaved Blue-Eyed Grass

Sisyrinchium angustifolium

IRIS FAMILY

These beautiful flowers can be found scattered among the grasses of moist meadows from low to the subalpine elevations. The distinctively flattened stems grow to 30 cm, and are twice as tall as the grass-like basal leaves. The blue flower is star-shaped, with three virtually identical petals and sepals, each tipped with a minute point. There is a bright-yellow eye in the centre. The blossoms are very short-lived, wilting usually within one day, to be replaced by fresh ones the next day.

Satin Flower (Grasswidow)

Olsynium douglasii

IRIS FAMILY

This beautiful species blooms very early in the spring in dry, open, rocky areas and in meadows and open woods that are seasonally wet in the spring but dry later in the year. The somewhat flattened stems grow up to 30 cm, taller than the grass-like basal leaves. The flowers, solitary to several, are bell-like, up to 3 cm wide, with six deep-reddish-purple tepals rounded at the ends. Inside the bell hang three yellow-tipped stamens and an elongated style that is three-pronged.

Chocolate Lily (Checker Lily)

Fritillaria affinis

LILY FAMILY

This early blooming upright perennial grows up to 80 cm tall in variable habitat that includes prairies, grassy bluffs, woodlands and conifer forests from sea level to the montane zone. The plant grows from a cluster of bulbs and small offsets that resemble grains of rice. The narrow, lance-shaped leaves are all borne on the stem, mostly arranged in one or two imperfect whorls of three to five leaves. Several foul-smelling nodding flowers occur in a loose raceme up the stem. Each individual flower has six purple tepals checked with yellow, giving the flower a dark-brown appearance.

Early Camas

Camassia quamash

LILY FAMILY

This plant of wet meadows and stream banks has long, narrow, grass-like leaves and a tall, naked stem. The startling blue to purplish flowers are numerous and appear in a loose cluster at the top of the stem. The flowers have six tepals that are spreading and somewhat unevenly spaced. The stamens are golden, and contrast vividly with the blue inflorescence of the plant. The bulbs were used as food by many Indigenous peoples and settlers. Large meadows containing the plants were closely guarded.

Harvest Brodiaea

Brodiaea coronaria

LILY FAMILY

This plant grows from a dark-brown, scaly, globe-shaped corm in dry meadows and grasslands. The corm puts up an erect, stout, leafless flowering stem that is up to 30 cm tall. There are one to three linear basal leaves that are almost as tall as the flowering stem, but they wither before the plant blooms. The funnel- to bell-shaped flowers are violet to purple with darker midlines on the petal centres, and occur in a loose umbel of up to ten erect to spreading blooms at the top of the stem.

Spanish Bluebell

Hyacinthoides hispanica

LILY FAMILY

This plant blooms in the spring in meadows and open woods, often forming extensive clumps of blue, pink and/or white flowers. The leaves are erect on emergence, but become floppy and tend to spread on the ground later in the blooming period. The inflorescence occurs as a loose spike of numerous flowers at the top of a bare stem. The flowers have six petals that are fused together at the base to form a wide, open bell. Each flower has two linear to lance-shaped bracts at the base of the flower stalk.

Bittersweet (Purple Nightshade)

Solanum dulcamara

NIGHTSHADE FAMILY

This plant is a Eurasian import that has become a noxious weed in many parts of North America, occurring most often in damp to wet thickets, clearings and open woods. It is a low, climbing, scrambling, sprawling vine that drapes itself over low trees and shrubs. The alternate, simple leaves are entire and broadly oval, with basal lobes. The flowers hang in loose clusters of up to 20 blooms. Each individual flower is star-shaped and up to 2 cm across, with five purple petals that are reflexed backward and yellow stamens and style pointing forward.

Large-Leafed Lupine (Bigleaf Lupine)

Lupinus polyphyllus

PEA FAMILY

This plant has erect stems that stand up to 150 cm tall in fields, along roadsides and in moist ground from low to montane elevations. The stems are usually unbranched, cylindrical and hollow at the base. The basal leaves are on long stalks, while the stem leaves are alternate and on shorter stalks. The leaves are palmately compound, with 9–17 elliptical leaflets that are pointed at the tip, smooth on top and sparsely hairy beneath. The inflorescence occurs at the top of the stem in a dense raceme of stalked, whorled and scattered bluish to violet pea-like flowers.

Jacob's Ladder (Showy Jacob's Ladder)

Polemonium pulcherrimum

PHLOX FAMILY

This plant grows in dry, open, rocky environments in the montane to alpine zones. The leaves are distinctive, being pinnately compound, with 11–25 leaflets that are evenly spaced, resembling a tiny ladder. The leaf arrangement gives the plant its common name, a reference to the story in the Book of Genesis of how Jacob found a ladder to heaven. The pale- to dark-blue, cup-shaped flowers appear in an open cluster at the top of the stem and have a vivid orange ring at the base of the cup. The plant has a foul odour.

Broad-Leaved Shooting Star (Few-Flowered Shooting Star)

Dodecatheon hendersonii

PRIMROSE FAMILY

This beautiful plant is scattered and locally common at low elevations in warm, dry, grassy meadows and open woods. Its basal leaves appear in a rosette and are egg-shaped, narrowing abruptly to the stalk. The numerous flowers appear nodding atop a leafless stalk. The flowers are purple to lavender with corolla lobes turned backwards. The stamens are united into a dark-purplish or black tube from which the style and anthers protrude. A harbinger of spring, these lovely flowers can bloom in huge numbers.

Purple Saxifrage (Purple Mountain Saxifrage)

Saxifraga oppositifolia

SAXIFRAGE FAMILY

This plant is a very low, matted, cushion-forming plant with tightly packed stems, common to rocky talus slopes, ledges and boulder fields in the alpine zone, particularly on calcium-rich substrates. The five-petalled purple to pink flowers appear singly on short stems. The opposite, stalkless leaves appear whorled. Each leaf is broadly wedge-shaped and bluish-green. Purple Saxifrage is the official flower of Nunavut.

Silky Phacelia (Silky Scorpionweed)

Phacelia sericea

WATERLEAF FAMILY

This spectacular plant grows on dry, rocky, open slopes at moderate to high elevations. The leaves are deeply divided into many segments and covered with silky hairs. The purple to blue flowers occur in clusters up a spike, resembling a bottle brush. The individual flowers are funnel-shaped, with long, purple, yellow-tipped stamens sticking out. The clusters of coiled branches resemble scorpion tails, thus the common name. The flowers of this plant are quite stunning, and having once seen them, one is unlikely to forget it.

Thread-Leaved Phacelia (Thread-Leaved Scorpionweed)

Phacelia linearis

WATERLEAF FAMILY

This annual species of *Phacelia* occurs in the southern part of the region, but is more common east of the coastal mountains. It grows to 50 cm tall, and appears on dry plateaus and foothills. Its hairy, alternate leaves are thin and linear below, developing side lobes higher on the stem. The lavender to blue flowers are reasonably large and appear in open clusters from the leaf axils.

Yellow Flowers

This section includes flowers that are predominantly yellow when encountered in the field. Their colour varies from bright yellow to pale cream. Some of the species included here have other colour variations, though, so you might have to check other parts of the book to find the one you're looking for. For example, the Paintbrushes (*Castilleja* sp) have a yellow variation but are most often encountered as red, so they are pictured in that section for purposes of sorting.

Skunk Cabbage (Yellow Arum)

Lysichiton americanum

ARUM FAMILY

This distinctive early-blooming perennial grows in large patches from a fleshy rhizome, inhabiting swamps, bogs, marshes and mucky ground at low to mid-elevations. The inflorescence appears before the leaves do, and consists of hundreds of tiny greenish-yellow flowers sunk into a thick, fleshy stalk known as a spadix, which is surrounded by a large, bright-yellow sheath leaf known as a spathe. The broadly elliptical leaves are huge, growing up to 120 cm long on stout stalks. The whole plant has an earthy odour, giving rise to the common name.

Oregon Grape

Mahonia nervosa

BARBERRY FAMILY

This evergreen shrub is widespread in the foothills, commonly at low to mid-elevations on dry plateaus and in dry to moist forests and openings. The plant very closely resembles holly, with shiny, sharp-pointed leaves that turn to lovely orange and rust colours in the fall. Its round flowers are pale to bright yellow, and bloom in the early spring, giving way to a small purple berry that resembles a grape.

Mountain Buttercup

Ranunculus eschscholtzii

BUTTERCUP FAMILY

This plant can reach heights of 30 cm and lives near or above timberline, appearing beside streams or ponds, near snowdrifts and around late snowmelt. The leaves are mainly basal, sometimes deeply lobed, and round to kidney-shaped. The flowering stems are hairless and may accommodate up to three flowers. The flowers are bright yellow, with five petals and five purple-tinged sepals. Stamens and pistils are numerous.

Footsteps of Spring (Snakeroot Sanicle)

Sanicula arctopoides

CARROT FAMILY

This perennial grows on coastal bluffs from a taproot, and has branching stems that are prostrate to ascending and up to 30 cm long. Its light-coloured, triangular basal leaves, which form a rosette on the ground, are deeply palmately three-cleft and up to 6 cm long and half again as wide. The inflorescence is several to many compact, dome-shaped umbels of tiny yellow flowers, each surrounded by a ring of long bracts which resemble the spokes of a wheel.

Canada Goldenrod

Solidago canadensis

COMPOSITE FAMILY

This upright perennial grows from a creeping rhizome and often forms large colonies in moist soil in meadows and along stream banks and lakeshores. Its solitary flowering stem is up to 1 m tall or more, has many branches near the top, and is covered with short, dense hairs. The simple, alternate leaves – all on the stem and relatively uniform in size – are lance-shaped to linear, sharply saw-toothed, and hairy. The tiny yellow flowers occur in dense, pyramid-shaped clusters at the tops of the stem branches. Each flower has yellow ray and disc florets.

Gumweed (Puget Sound Gumweed)

Grindelia integrifolia

COMPOSITE FAMILY

This perennial herb grows from a taproot, with several erect to ascending stems that are usually branched and up to 80 cm tall. The plant occurs at the edges of salt marshes, along rocky shores and in open meadows at low elevations. The stem leaves are small, unstalked, and somewhat clasping. The inflorescence is solitary composite heads at the tops of the stems, consisting of yellow ray flowers surrounding yellow disc flowers. Under the flower heads are slender, green-tipped, sticky bracts that give the plant its common name.

Heart-Leaved Arnica

Arnica cordifolia

COMPOSITE FAMILY

Arnica is a common plant of wooded areas in the mountains, foothills and boreal forest. The leaves occur in two to four opposite pairs along the stem, each with long stalks and heart-shaped, serrated blades. The uppermost pair is stalkless and more lance-shaped than the lower leaves. The flowers have 10–15 bright-yellow ray florets and bright-yellow central disc florets.

Pale Agoseris (False Dandelion)

Agoseris glauca

COMPOSITE FAMILY

This common plant shares many characteristics with the dandelions, including a long taproot, a rosette of basal leaves, a leafless stem, a single yellow flower appearing on a long stalk and the production of a sticky, milky juice that is apparent when the stem is broken. This flower is often passed over as just another dandelion, but upon closer examination several differences are notable. Agoseris is generally a taller plant than dandelion; its leaves are longer; and the leaf blades are smooth or faintly toothed rather than deeply incised.

Pineapple Weed (Disc Mayweed)

Matricaria discoidea

COMPOSITE FAMILY

This branching annual grows up to 40 cm tall along roadsides, in ditches and on disturbed ground. The stem leaves are alternate and fern-like, with finely dissected, narrow segments. Basal leaves have usually fallen off by the time flowering occurs. The flowers are several to many composite heads, with greenish to yellow disc florets on a cone- or dome-shaped base. There are no ray florets. When crushed, the leaves and flowers of the plant produce a distinctive pineapple aroma, hence the common name.

Smooth Hawksbeard

Crepis capillaria

COMPOSITE FAMILY

This European native was introduced into the region, and now occurs along roadsides and in meadows, pastures and disturbed areas. It grows from a short taproot, sending up a solitary, many-branched, short-hairy stem that is up to 90 cm tall. The stem leaves are lance-shaped, clasping and pointed. The yellow flowers appear in heads in flat or round-topped clusters. The strap-shaped individual flowers are unstalked and composed entirely of ray florets. The fruits are round-ribbed, brownish achenes with a short beak at the end.

Sow Thistle (Perennial Sow Thistle)

Sonchus arvensis

COMPOSITE FAMILY

This is a plant of cultivated fields, roadsides, ditches and pastures. Its flowers have large yellow ray florets similar to dandelion flowers. Sow Thistle is an imported species from Europe and is not a true thistle. Sow Thistles will exude a milky latex when the stem is crushed, while true thistles do not. The common name is derived from the fact that pigs like to eat this plant.

Spear-Head Senecio (Arrow-Leaved Ragwort)

Senecio triangularis

COMPOSITE FAMILY

This lush, leafy perennial herb often grows to 150 cm tall and occurs in large clumps in moist to wet open or partly shaded sites from foothills to alpine elevations. The leaves are alternate, spearhead or arrowhead-shaped, squared off at the base and tapered to a point. The leaves are numerous and well developed along the whole stem. The flowers occur in flat-topped clusters at the top of the plant and have five to eight bright-yellow ray florets surrounding a disc of bright-yellow to orange florets.

Tansy
Tanacetum vulgare

COMPOSITE FAMILY

This plant was introduced from Europe and is common in pastures and disturbed areas and along roadsides, embankments and fences. Its flattened yellow flowers occur in numerous bunches atop multiple stalks and resemble buttons. The dark green, finely dissected leaves are fern-like and strong smelling. During the Middle Ages a posy of Tansy was thought, fancifully, to ward off the Black Death.

Woolly Sunflower (Oregon Sunshine)
Eriophyllum lanatum

COMPOSITE FAMILY

This perennial grows up to 60 cm tall in dry, open, rocky areas from seaside to mid-elevations. The plant usually grows in clumps and is white-woolly throughout. The basal leaves are few and usually wilt before blooming commences. The stem leaves are alternate to opposite, smooth on the margins or narrowly lobed and up to 8 cm long. The flowers are solitary atop the stems, with flower heads consisting of 8–13 yellow ray flowers up to 2 cm long and yellow disc flowers.

Bracted Lousewort (Wood Betony)

Pedicularis bracteosa

FIGWORT FAMILY

This plant can attain heights of up to 1 m and is found at subalpine and alpine elevations in moist forests, meadows and clearings. Its fern-like leaves are divided into long, narrow, toothed segments and are attached to the upper portions of the stem of the plant. The flowers, varying from yellow to red to purple, arise from the axils of leafy bracts and occur in an elongated cluster at the top of the stem. They have a two-lipped corolla, giving the impression of a bird's beak.

Butter and Eggs (Toadflax)

Linaria vulgaris

FIGWORT FAMILY

This is a common plant of roadsides, ditches, fields and disturbed areas that grows up to 1 m tall. Its dark-green leaves are alternate and narrow. The bright-yellow, orange-throated flowers are similar in shape to snapdragons and occur in dense terminal clusters at the tops of erect stems. The corolla is spurred at the base and two-lipped, the upper lip having two lobes, the lower one, three. The common name arises from the yellow and orange tones on the flowers, reminiscent of butter and eggs.

Common Mullein
Verbascum thapsis

FIGWORT FAMILY

This Eurasian import is quite common along roadsides, in gravelly places and on dry slopes. The plant is a biennial, taking two years to produce flowers. In the first year, it puts out a rosette of large leaves that are very soft to the touch, much like velvet or flannel. A strong, sentinel-like stalk appears in the second year. The small yellow flowers appear randomly on the flowering spike. At no time do all the flowers bloom together. After flowering, the dead stalk turns dark brown and may persist for many months.

Little Monkeyflower (Chickweed Monkeyflower)
Mimulus alsinoides

FIGWORT FAMILY

This plant occurs, often in large patches, in moist, sheltered, rocky areas at low elevations. Its stems are freely branching and smooth to slightly hairy. The stalked, egg-shaped leaves are opposite and irregularly toothed. The flowers are tubular in construction, have long stalks, and appear in the axils of the leaves, usually in pairs. The flowers are two-lipped, with the upper lip having two lobes, the lower one, three. The middle lobe on the lower lip has a characteristic red blotch at its base. The markings typically give the appearance of a grinning face.

Yellow Monkeyflower

Mimulus guttatus

FIGWORT FAMILY

This plant occurs, often in large patches, along streams, at seeps and in moist meadows. The species is quite variable, but is always spectacular when found. The bright-yellow flowers resemble snapdragons, and occur in clusters. The flowers usually have red or purple dots on the lip, giving the appearance of a grinning face. The genus name, *Mimulus*, is derived from the Latin *mimus*, meaning "mimic" or "actor."

Yellow Sand Verbena

Abronia latifolia

FOUR O'CLOCK FAMILY

This perennial grows from a deep taproot in loose, shifting beach sand along the coast, away from the surf. The plant is glandular hairy and sticky throughout, and its stems trail up to 2 m long, often forming dense mats. Its thick, fleshy leaves are oval and opposite. The inflorescence occurs in rounded heads (umbels) on stout stalks that are up to 6 cm tall. The umbel contains up to 35 flowers, each a yellow tube with a flared mouth that is divided into five lobes.

Yellow Heather (Yellow Mountain Heather)

Phyllodoce glanduliflora

HEATH FAMILY

This is a dwarf evergreen shrub that grows up to 30 cm tall and thrives in subalpine and alpine meadows and slopes near timberline. Its flowers, stems and new growth are covered with small sticky hairs. The blunt, needle-like leaves are grooved on their undersides. The yellowish-green, vase- or urn-shaped flowers are nodding in clusters at the tops of the stems.

Black Twinberry (Bracted Honeysuckle)

Lonicera involucrata

HONEYSUCKLE FAMILY

This plant is a shrub that grows up to 2 m tall in moist woods and along stream banks. Its yellow flowers occur in pairs arising from the axils of the leaves, and are overlain by a purple to reddish leafy bract. As the fruit ripens the bract remains, enlarges and darkens in colour. The ripe fruits occur in pairs and are black. They are bitter to the taste, but serve as food for a variety of birds and small mammals.

Glacier Lily (Yellow Avalanche Lily)

Erythronium grandiflorum

LILY FAMILY

This gorgeous lily is one of the first blooms in the spring, often appearing at the edges of receding snowbanks on mountain slopes, thus the common names. The bright-yellow flowers appear at the top of a leafless stem, usually solitary, though a plant might have up to three flowers. The flowers are nodding, with six tepals that are tapered to the tip and reflexed, with white, yellow or brown anthers. The broadly oblong, glossy leaves, usually two, are attached near the base of the stem and are unmarked.

Bird's Foot Trefoil

Lotus corniculatus

PEA FAMILY

This is a low-growing, sprawling, creeping perennial that was introduced from Europe, where it was a pasture plant. Since its arrival, it has spread extensively over the region. It is usually prostrate, but can put up stems 20 cm tall. The leaves are hairless and trifoliate, typical of the pea family. The flowers are yellow, often tinged with red, and occur in a head of three to a dozen individual flowers in a cluster at the ends of bare stems, reminiscent of clover blooms.

Bog Bird's Foot Trefoil

Lotus pinnatus

PEA FAMILY

This native perennial grows from a thick taproot in wet to moist meadows and along streams at low elevations. Its hollow, sparsely hairy stems are sprawling to erect and up to 60 cm long. The leaves are pinnately compound with five to nine elliptical to egg-shaped leaflets. The inflorescence occurs on a long stem that arises from the leaf axil and consists of a compact umbel of 3–12 pea-like flowers. The banner and keel on each flower are yellow, the wings white.

Gorse

Ulex europaeus

PEA FAMILY

This non-native spiny evergreen shrub can be up to 2 m tall in open areas and on disturbed ground from the coast to low mountains. The plant grows from a creeping rhizome as well as from seed distribution, making it a formidable invader that forces out native vegetation quickly and efficiently. Its leaves are simple, stiff and up to 15 mm long. This species only has the typical trifoliate pea-shaped leaves as a seedling. Its shiny yellow flowers, however, are typical of the pea family.

Scotch Broom (Broom)

Cytisus scoparius

PEA FAMILY

This non-native shrub grows up to 3 m tall in open and disturbed ground from the coast to low mountains. The plant grows from a creeping rhizome as well as seed distribution, making it aggressively invasive. Its lower leaves have the typical trifoliate pea shape but are undivided above. The flowers are shiny yellow, sometimes tinged with purple or red, as is typical of the pea family, occurring one per leaf axil. The fruits are purplish-brown legumes which open explosively when ripe, casting seeds some distance from the parent plant.

California Poppy

Eschscholzia californica

POPPY FAMILY

This familiar perennial is easily recognized by its saucer-shaped, four petalled, orange-yellow flowers atop smooth stems that are up to 30 cm tall. The plant grows from a deep taproot, and puts up one to several flowering stems that are spreading to erect. The basal leaves are blue-green, triangular in shape and three times divided into three leaflets. The plant has extended its range northward over time and is now naturalized in Washington and British Columbia.

Yellow Mountain Avens (Drummond's Mountain Avens)

Dryas drummondii

ROSE FAMILY

This is a plant of gravelly streams and riverbanks, slopes and roadsides in foothills and mountains. The yellow flower is solitary and nodding, with black, glandular hairs, blooming on the top of a hairy, leafless stalk. Leaves are alternate, leathery and wrinkly, dark-green above and whitish-hairy beneath. The fruit consists of many achenes, each with a silky, feathery, golden-yellow plume that becomes twisted around the others into a tight spiral that later opens into a fluffy mass, dispersing the seeds on the wind.

Large-Leaved Avens

Geum macrophyllum

ROSE FAMILY

This is a tall, erect, hairy perennial that grows in moist woods, along rivers and streams and in thickets from low to subalpine elevations. Its bright-yellow flowers are saucer-shaped, with five petals, usually appearing at the tip of a tall, slender stem. The basal leaves occur in a cluster. The terminal leaf is rounded, shallowly lobed and much larger than the lateral leaves below. The fruits are achenes that have hooks on them which will cling to the clothing of passersby and the fur of animals as a seed dispersal mechanism.

Sibbaldia

Sibbaldia procumbens

ROSE FAMILY

This is a ground-hugging alpine-zone perennial that forms cushions. Its prostrate stems branch from the base and terminate in clusters of three leaflets, similar to clover. White hairs cover both surfaces of the leaflets. The pale-yellow flowers are generally saucer-shaped and appear in clusters at the tops of the flowering stems. Each flower is made up of five yellow petals that alternate with five hairy green sepals. The petals are about half as long as the sepals.

Silverweed

Potentilla anserina

ROSE FAMILY

This plant is a low, prostrate perennial that grows from thick rootstock and reddish-coloured runners in moist meadows and on riverbanks, lakeshores and slough margins. The leaves are basal, compound, toothed and pinnate, with 7–25 leaflets per leaf. Each silky-haired leaflet is green to silvery on top, lighter underneath. The flowers are bright yellow and solitary on leafless stems, with rounded petals in fives. The sepals are light green and hairy, and appear between the petals.

Western St. John's Wort

Hypericum scouleri
(also *H. formosum*)

ST. JOHN'S WORT FAMILY

This perennial appears in moist places from foothills to the alpine zone and grows to 25 cm tall. The leaves are opposite, egg-shaped to elliptical, 1–3 cm long, somewhat clasping at the base, and usually have purplish-black dots along the edges. The bright-yellow flowers have five petals and occur in open clusters at the top of the plant. The stamens are numerous, often resembling a starburst.

Lance-Leaved Stonecrop (Spearleaf Stonecrop)

Sedum lanceolatum

STONECROP FAMILY

This fleshy perennial with reddish stems grows up to 15 cm tall on dry, rocky, open slopes and in meadows and rock crevices from low elevations to above timberline. Its numerous, fleshy, alternate leaves are round in cross-section, overlapping and mostly basal. The bright-yellow flowers are star-shaped with sharp-pointed petals, and occur in dense, flat-topped clusters atop short stems.

Yellow Wood Violet

Viola glabella

VIOLET FAMILY

This beautiful yellow violet occurs in moist woods, often in extensive patches. There are smooth, serrate, heart-shaped leaves on the upper part of the plant stem. The flowers have very short spurs, and the interior of the side petals often exhibits a white beard. The flower is also commonly referred to as Smooth Violet and Stream Violet.

Yellow Pond Lily (Yellow Water Lily)

Nuphar variegatum

WATER LILY FAMILY

This aquatic perennial found in ponds, lakes and slow-moving streams is perhaps the most recognizable water plant in the region. It grows from a thick rootstock, producing cord-like stems. The floating leaves, up to 15 cm long, are borne singly on long stems. They are waxy on the surface, round and broadly oval, and heart-shaped at the base. The large flowers protrude from the water's surface, as solitary on a long stalk.

GLOSSARY

achene: A dry, single-seeded fruit that does not split open at maturity.

alternate: A reference to the arrangement of leaves on a stem where the leaves appear singly and staggered on opposite sides of the stem.

annual: A plant that completes its life cycle, from seed germination to production of new seed, within one year and then dies.

anther: The portion of the stamen (the male portion of a flower) that produces pollen.

axil: The upper angle formed where a leaf, branch or other organ is attached to a plant stem.

basal: A reference to leaves that occur at the bottom of the plant, usually near or on the ground.

berry: A fleshy, many-seeded fruit.

biennial: A plant that completes its life cycle in two years, normally producing leaves in the first year and flowers in the second, before dying.

blade: The body of a leaf, excluding the stalk.

bract: A reduced or otherwise modified leaf that is usually found near the flower of a plant but is not part of the flower. *See also* **florescence**; **inflorescence**.

bulb: An underground plant part derived from a short, often rounded shoot that is covered with scales or leaves.

calyx: The outer set of flower parts, usually composed of sepals.

capsule: A dry fruit with more than one compartment that splits open to release seeds.

clasping: In reference to a leaf that surrounds or partially wraps around a stem or branch.

composite inflorescence: A flower-like **inflorescence** of the Composite Family, made up of **ray flowers** and/or **disc flowers**. Where both ray and disc flowers exist, the ray flowers surround the disc flowers.

compound leaf: A leaf that is divided into two or many leaflets, each of which may look like a complete leaf but lacks buds. Compound leaves may have a variety of arrangements.

connate: In reference to leaves where two leaves are fused at their bases to form a shallow cup, often seen in the Honeysuckle Family.

corm: An enlarged base or stem resembling a bulb.

corolla: The collective term for the petals of the flower that are found inside the sepals.

cultivar: A cultivated variety of a wild plant.

cyme: A broad, flat-topped flower arrangement in which the inner, central flowers bloom first.

decumbent: In reference to a plant reclining, or lying on the ground with tip ascending.

disc flower: Any of the small tubular florets found in the central, clustered portion of the flower head of members of the Composite Family; also referred to as "disc florets."

dioecious: Having unisex flowers, where male and female flowers appear on separate plants. *See also* **monoecious.**

drupe: A fleshy or juicy fruit that covers a single, stony seed inside, e.g., a cherry or a peach.

drupelet: Any one part of an aggregate fruit (like a raspberry or blackberry), where each such part is a fleshy fruit that covers a single, stony seed inside.

elliptical: Ellipse-shaped, widest in the middle. *See also* **oval.**

elongate: Having a slender form, long in relation to width.

entire: In reference to a leaf edge that is smooth, without teeth or notches.

filament: The part of the stamen that supports the anther. Also can refer to any threadlike structure.

florescence: Generally the flowering part of a plant; the arrangement of the flowers on the stem; also referred to as **inflorescence.** *But see* **bract.**

floret: One of the small tubular flowers in the central, clustered portion of the flower head of members of the Composite Family; also known as **disc flower.**

follicle: A dry fruit composed of a single compartment that splits open along one side at maturity to release seeds.

fruit: The ripe ovary with the enclosed seeds, and any other structures that enclose it.

glabrous: In reference to a leaf surface, smooth, neither waxy or sticky.

gland: A small organ that secretes a sticky or oily substance and is attached to some part of the plant.

glaucous: Having a fine, waxy, often white coating that may be rubbed off; often characteristic of leaves, fruits and stems.

hood: in reference to flower structure, a curving or folded petal-like structure interior to the petals and exterior to the stamens in certain flowers.

host: In reference to a parasitic or semi-parasitic plant, the plant from which the parasite obtains its nourishment.

inflorescence: Generally the flowering part of a plant; the arrangement of the flowers on the stem; also referred to as **florescence.** *But see* **bract.**

keel: The two fused petals in flowers that are members of the Pea Family.

lance-shaped: In reference to leaf shape, much longer than wide, widest below the middle and tapering to the tip, like the blade of a lance.

leaflet: A distinct, leaflike segment of a compound leaf.

linear: Like a line; long, narrow and parallel-sided.

lobe: A reference to the arrangement of leaves, a segment of a divided plant part, typically rounded.

margin: The edge of a leaf or petal.

mat: A densely interwoven or tangled, low, ground-hugging growth.

midrib: The main rib of a leaf.

mid-vein : The middle vein of a leaf.

monoecious: A plant having unisex flowers, with separate male and female flowers on the same plant. *See also* **dioecious.**

nectary: A plant structure that produces and secretes nectar.

node: A joint on a stem or root.

noxious weed: A plant, usually imported, that out-competes and drives out native plants.

oblong: Somewhat rectangular, with rounded ends.

obovate: Shaped like a teardrop.

opposite: A reference to the arrangement of leaves on a stem where the leaves appear paired on opposite sides of the stem, directly across from each other.

oval: Broadly elliptical.

ovary: The portion of the flower where the seeds develop. It is usually a swollen area below the style and stigma.

ovate: Egg-shaped.

palmate: A reference to the arrangement of leaves on a stem where the leaves spread like the fingers on a hand, diverging from a central or common point.

panicle: A branched inflorescence that blooms from the bottom up.

pencilled: Marked with coloured lines, like the petals on Violets.

perennial: A plant that does not produce seeds or flowers until its second year of life, then lives for three or more years, usually flowering each year before dying.

petal: A component of the inner floral portion of a flower, often the most brightly coloured and visible part of the flower.

petiole: The stem of a leaf.

pinnate: A reference to the arrangement of leaves on a stem where the leaves appear in two rows on opposite sides of a central stem, similar to the construction of a feather.

pistil: The female member of a flower that produces seed, consisting of the ovary, the style and the stigma. A flower may have one to several separate pistils.

pistillate: A flower with female reproductive parts but no male reproductive parts.

pollen: The tiny, often powdery male reproductive microspores formed in the stamens and necessary for sexual reproduction in flowering plants.

pome: A fruit with a core, e.g., an apple or pear.

prickle: A small, sharp, spiny outgrowth from the outer surface.

raceme: A flower arrangement that has an elongated flower cluster with the flowers attached to short stalks of relatively equal length that are attached to the main central stalk.

ray flower: One of the outer, strap-shaped petals seen in members of the Composite Family. Ray flowers may surround disc flowers or may comprise the whole of the flower head; also referred to as **ray florets**.

reflexed: Bent backwards, often in reference to petals, bracts or stalks.

rhizome: An underground stem that produces roots and shoots at the nodes.

rosette: A dense cluster of basal leaves from a common underground part, often in a flattened, circular arrangement.

runner: A long, trailing or creeping stem.

saprophyte: An organism that obtains its nutrients from dead organic matter.

scape: A flowering stem, usually leafless, rising from the crown, roots or corm of a plant. Scapes can have a single or many flowers.

sepal: A leaf-like appendage that surrounds the petals of a flower. Collectively the sepals make up the calyx.

serrate: Possessing sharp, forward-pointing teeth.

sessile: Of a plant structure attached directly by its base without a stalk; opposite of "stalked."

shrub: A multi-stemmed woody plant.

simple leaf: A leaf that has a single leaf-like blade, which may be lobed or divided.

spadix: A floral spike with a fleshy or succulent axis usually enclosed in a **spathe**.

spathe: A sheathing **bract** or pair of bracts partly enclosing an inflorescence and especially a **spadix** on the same axis.

spike: An elongated, unbranched cluster of stalkless or nearly stalkless flowers.

spine: A thin, stiff, sharp-pointed projection.

spur: A hollow, tubular projection arising from the base of a petal or sepal, often producing nectar.

stalk: The stem supporting the leaf, flower or flower cluster.

stamen: The male member of the flower, which produces pollen; the structure typically consists of an anther and a filament.

staminate: A flower with male reproductive parts but no female reproductive parts

staminode: A sterile stamen.

standard: The uppermost petal of a typical flower in the Pea Family.

stigma: The portion of the pistil receptive to pollination; usually at the top of the style and often sticky or fuzzy.

stolon: A creeping above-ground stem capable of sending up a new plant.

style: A slender stalk connecting the stigma to the ovary in the female organ of a flower.

taproot: A stout main root that extends downward.

tendril: A slender, coiled or twisted filament with which climbing plants attach to their supports.

tepals: Petals and sepals that cannot be distinguished, one from the other.

terminal: At the top of, such as of a stem or other appendage.

terminal flower head: A flower that appears at the top of a stem, as opposed to originating from a leaf axil.

ternate: Arranged in threes, often in reference to leaf structures.

toothed: Bearing teeth or sharply angled projections along the edge.

trailing: Lying flat on the ground but not rooting.

tuber: A thick, creeping underground stem.

tubular: Hollow or cylindrical, usually in reference to a fused corolla.

umbel: A flower arrangement where the flower stalks have a common point of attachment to the stem, like the spokes of an umbrella.

unisexual: Some flowers are unisexual, having either male parts or female parts but not both. Some plants are unisexual, having either male flowers or female flowers but not both.

urn-shaped: Hollow and cylindrical or globular, contracted at the mouth; like an urn.

vacuole: A membrane-bound compartment in a plant that is typically filled with liquid and may perform various functions in the plant.

vein: A small tube that carries water, nutrients and minerals, usually referring to leaves.

viscid: Sticky, thick and gluey.

whorl: Three or more parts attached at the same point along a stem or axis, often surrounding the stem; forming a ring radiating out from a common point.

wings: Side petals that flank the keel in typical flowers of the Pea Family.

INDEX

Abronia latifolia   80

Achlys triphylla   28

Aconitum columbianum   58

Actaea rubra   30

Adenocaulon bicolor   36

Agoseris aurantiaca   4

Agoseris glauca   4, 74

Agrimonia striata   66

Alaska Rein Orchid   45

Allium acuminatum   18

Allium cernuum   19

Alpine Speedwell   60

Alpine Veronica. *See* Alpine Speedwell

Anagallis arvensis   23

Anaphalis margaritacea   36

Androsace chamaejasme   49

Anemone lyallii   30

Anemone occidentalis. *See* Pulsatilla occidentalis

Antennaria microphylla   5

Apocynum androsaemifolium   6

Aquilegia formosa   3

Arctostaphylos uva-ursi   10

Arnica cordifolia   74

Arrow-Leaved Ragwort. *See* Spear-Head Senecio

Arum Family
Skunk Cabbage   71

Asarum canadense   2

Baldhip Rose. *See* Dwarf Woodland Rose

Baneberry   30

Barberry Family
Oregon Grape   71
Vanilla Leaf   28

Bare-Stemmed Mitrewort. *See* Bishop's Cap

Beach Pea   22

Beadlily. *See* Queen's Cup

Bearberry   10

Beaver Poison. *See* Water Hemlock

Bell-Bind. *See* Morning Glory

Bigleaf Lupine. *See* Large-Leafed Lupine

Bird's Foot Trefoil   82

Birthwort Family
Wild Ginger   2

Bishop's Cap   53

Bittersweet   66

Bittersweet Family
Falsebox   2

Black Huckleberry   11

Black Twinberry   81

Bladderwort Family
Common Butterwort   57

Bluebead Lily. *See* Queen's Cup

Blue Sailors   59

Bog Bird's Foot Trefoil   83

Bog Cranberry   11

Borage Family
Forget-Me-Not   57

Bracted Honeysuckle. *See* Black Twinberry

Bracted Lousewort   78

Broad-Leaved Shooting Star   68

Broad-Leaved Willowherb. *See* River Beauty

Brodiaea coronaria   65

Bronzebells   41

Broom. *See* Scotch Broom

Buckbrush   28

Buckthorn Family
  Buckbrush   28

Buckwheat Family
  Mountain Sorrel   29
  Sulphur Buckwheat   29
  Water Smartweed   3

Bull Thistle   4

Bunchberry   37

Butter and Eggs   78

Buttercup Family
  Baneberry   30
  False Bugbane   31
  Globeflower   31
  Lyall's Anemone   30
  Menzies Larkspur   58
  Monkshood   58
  Mountain Buttercup   72
  Mountain Marsh Marigold   32
  Red Columbine   3
  Western Anemone   32

California Poppy   84

Caltha leptosepala   32

Calypso bulbosa   20

Calystegia sepium   45

Camassia quamash   65

Campanula rotundifolia   63

Canada Goldenrod   73

Carolina Bugbane. *See* False Bugbane

Carrot Family
  Chocolate Tips   33
  Cow Parsnip   33
  Footsteps of Spring   72
  Queen Anne's Lace   34
  Water Hemlock   34

Castilleja miniata   9

Ceanothus sanguineus   28

Cerastium arvense   48

Chalice Flower. *See* Western Anemone

Chamaenerion angustifolium   7

Chamaenerion latifolium   7

Checker Lily. *See* Chocolate Lily

Chickweed Monkeyflower. *See* Little Monkeyflower

Chicory. *See* Blue Sailors

Children's Bane. *See* Water Hemlock

Chimaphila umbellata   14

Chocolate Lily   64

Chocolate Tips   33

Cichorium intybus   59

Cicuta douglasii. See C. maculata

Cicuta maculata   34

Cirsium vulgare   4

Clasping-Leaved Twisted-Stalk   42

Claytonia lanceolata   49

Clintonia uniflora   43

Collinsia parviflora   61

Columbia Lily. *See* Tiger Lily

Common Butterwort   57

Common Mullein   79

Composite Family
  Blue Sailors   59
  Bull Thistle   4
  Canada Goldenrod   73
  Daisy Fleabane   35
  Gumweed   73
  Heart-Leaved Arnica   74
  Orange Agoseris   4
  Orange Hawkweed   5
  Ox-Eye Daisy   35
  Oyster Plant   59
  Pale Agoseris   74
  Pathfinder Plant   36
  Pearly Everlasting   36
  Pineapple Weed   75
  Pink Pussytoes   5
  Smooth Hawksbeard   75

Sow Thistle   76
Spear-Head Senecio   76
Tall Purple Fleabane   60
Tansy   77
Woolly Sunflower   77

Convolvulus sepium. See Calystegia sepium

Corallorhiza maculata   21

Corallorhiza striata   21

Cornus canadensis   37

Cornus nuttallii   37

Cow Parsnip   33

Cream Bush. *See* Ocean Spray

Creeping Spiraea. *See* Partridgefoot

Crepis capillaria   75

Currant Family
Flowering Red Currant   6

Cut-Leaf Daisy. *See* Daisy Fleabane

Cypripedium montanum   47

Cytisus scoparius   84

Daisy Fleabane   35

Daucus carota   34

Death of Man. *See* Water Hemlock

Delphinium menziesii   58

Dicentra flormosa   9

Digitalis purpurea   8

Disc Mayweed. *See* Pineapple Weed

Disporum hookeri. See Prosartes hookeri

Dodecatheon pulchellum   68

Dogbane Family
Spreading Dogbane   6

Dogwood Family
Bunchberry   37
Pacific Dogwood   37

Douglas Spirea. *See* Hardhack

Drosera rotundifolia   55

Drummond's Mountain Avens. *See* Yellow Mountain Avens

Dryas drummondii   85

Dryas octopetala   52

Dutch Clover. *See* White Clover

Dwarf Dogwood. *See* Bunchberry

Dwarf Fireweed. *See* River Beauty

Dwarf Raspberry   24

Dwarf Woodland Rose   24

Early Camas   65

Epilobium angustifolium. See Chamaenerion angustifolium

Epilobium latifolium. See Chamaenerion latifolium

Erigeron compositus   35

Erigeron peregrinus   60

Eriogonum ovalifolium   29

Eriophyllum lanatum   77

Erythronium grandiflorum   82

Erythronium oregonum   44

Erythronium revolutum   19

Eschscholzia californica   84

Evening Primrose Family
Fireweed   7
River Beauty   7

Fairybells   42

Fairy Slipper. *See* Venus Slipper

False Azalea   12

Falsebox   2

False Bugbane   31

False Dandelion. *See* Orange Agoseris; *See* Pale Agoseris

False Mitrewort. *See* Foamflower

Fern-Leaved Desert Parsley. *See* Chocolate Tips

Few-Flowered Shooting Star. *See* Broad-Leaved Shooting Star

Field Chickweed. *See* Mouse-Ear Chickweed

Figwort Family
Alpine Speedwell   60
Bracted Lousewort   78
Butter and Eggs   78
Common Mullein   79
Foxglove   8

Little Monkeyflower   79
Red Monkeyflower   8
Red Paintbrush   9
Sickletop Lousewort   38
Slender Speedwell   61
Small-Flowered Blue-Eyed Mary   61
Small-Flowered Penstemon   62
Yellow Monkeyflower   80

Fireweed   7

Flowering Red Currant   6

Foamflower   53

Fool's Huckleberry. *See* **False Azalea**

Footsteps of Spring   72

Forget-Me-Not   57

Four O'Clock Family
Yellow Sand Verbena   80

Foxglove   8

Fritillaria affinis   64

Fumitory Family
Wild Bleeding Heart   9

Gaultheria shallon   15

Gentiana amarella. See Gentianella amarella

Gentianella amarella   62

Gentian Family
Northern Gentian   62

Geranium Family
Herb Robert   10

Geranium robertianum   10

Geum macrophyllum   85

Glacier Lily   82

Globeflower   31

Goodyera oblongifolia   47

Gorse   83

Grasswidow. *See* **Satin Flower**

Great Willowherb. *See* **Fireweed**

Greenish-Flowered Wintergreen   38

Green Wintergreen. *See* **Greenish-Flow-ered Wintergreen**

Grindelia integrifolia   73

Gumweed   73

Hardhack   25

Harebell   63

Harebell Family
Harebell   63

Harvest Brodiaea   65

Heart-Leaved Arnica   74

Heart-Leaved Twayblade   46

Heath Family
Bearberry   10
Black Huckleberry   11
Bog Cranberry   11
False Azalea   12
Greenish-Flowered Wintergreen   38
One-Sided Wintergreen   39
Oval-Leaved Blueberry   12
Pine-Drops   13
Pink Rhododendron   13
Pink Wintergreen   14
Pipsissewa   14
Red Heather   15
Salal   15
Single Delight   39
Swamp Laurel   16
White Rhododendron   40
Yellow Heather   81

Hedge Bindweed. *See* **Morning Glory**

Hedge Nettle   20

Heracleum lanatum   33

Herb Robert   10

Hieracium aurantiacum   5

"Hippies on a Stick". *See* **Western Anemone**

Holodiscus discolor   50

Honeysuckle Family
Black Twinberry   81
Orange Honeysuckle   16
Red Twinberry   40
Snowberry   17
Twinflower   17

Hooded Ladies' Tresses   46

Hooker's Onion   18

Hydrangea Family
Mock Orange   41

Hypericum formosum. See H. scouleri

Hypericum scouleri 87

Indian Plum 50

Iris Family
    Narrow-Leaved Blue-Eyed Grass 63
    Satin Flower 64

Jacob's Ladder 67

Kalmia microphylla 16

Kinnikinnick. *See* Bearberry

Lady's Nightcap. *See* Morning Glory

Lance-Leaved Stonecrop 87

Large-Leafed Lupine 67

Large-Leaved Avens 85

Lathyrus japonicus 22

Lathyrus latifolius 22

Lathyrus maritina. See L. japonicus

Leafy Lousewort. *See* Sickletop
    Lousewort

Leather-Leaved Saxifrage 54

Leptarrhena pyrolifolia 54

Leucanthemum vulgare 35

Lewis's Monkeyflower. *See* Red
    Monkeyflower

Lilium columbianum 18

Lily Family
    Bronzebells 41
    Chocolate Lily 64
    Clasping-Leaved Twisted-Stalk 42
    Early Camas 65
    Fairybells 42
    Glacier Lily 82
    Harvest Brodiaea 65
    Hooker's Onion 18
    Nodding Onion 19
    Pink Fawn Lily 19
    Queen's Cup 43
    Spanish Bluebell 66
    Star-Flowered Solomon's-Seal 43
    Tiger Lily 18
    Western Trillium 44
    White Fawn Lily 44

Linaria vulgaris 78

Linnaea borealis 17

Listera cordata 46

Little Monkeyflower 79

Lomatium dissectum 33

Lonicera ciliosa 16

Lonicera involucrata 81

Lonicera utahensis 40

Lotus corniculatus 82

Lotus pinnatus 83

Luetkea pectinata 51

Lupinus polyphyllus 67

Lyall's Anemone 30

Lysichiton americanum 71

Mahonia nervosa 71

Maianthemum stellatum 43

Matricaria discoidea 75

Menziesia ferruginea 12

Menzies Larkspur 58

Mimulus alsinoides 79

Mimulus guttatus 80

Mimulus lewisii 8

Mint Family
    Hedge Nettle 20

Mitella nuda 53

Mock Orange 41

Moneses uniflora 39

Monkshood 58

Morning Glory 45

Morning Glory Family
    Morning Glory 45

Mountain Boxwood 2

Mountain Buttercup 72

Mountain Lady's Slipper 47

Mountain-Lover 2

Mountain Marsh Marigold 32

Mountain Sorrel 29

Mouse-Ear Chickweed 48

Myosotis laxa 57

Narrow-Leaved Blue-Eyed Grass 63

Nightshade Family
  Bittersweet   66

Nodding Onion   19

Nootka Rose   25

Northern Gentian   62

Nuphar variegata   88

Ocean Spray   50

Oemleria cerasiformis   50

Olsynium douglasii   64

One-Flowered Wintergreen. See Single Delight

One-Sided Wintergreen   39

Orange Agoseris   4

Orange-Flowered False Dandelion. See Orange Agoseris

Orange Hawkweed   5

Orange Honeysuckle   16

Orchid Family
  Alaska Rein Orchid   45
  Heart-Leaved Twayblade   46
  Hooded Ladies' Tresses   46
  Mountain Lady's Slipper   47
  Spotted Coralroot   21
  Striped Coralroot   21
  Venus Slipper   20
  Western Rattlesnake Plantain   47

Oregon Boxwood   2

Oregon Grape   71

Oregon Sunshine. See Woolly Sunflower

Orthilia secunda. See Pyrola secunda

Osoberry. See Indian Plum

Oval-Leaved Blueberry   12

Ox-Eye Daisy   35

Oxycoccus oxycoccus. See Vaccinium oxycoccos

Oxyria digyn   29

Oyster Plant   59

Pacific Dogwood   37

Pacific Ninebark   51

Pale Agoseris   74

Parrot's Beak. See Sickletop Lousewort

Partridgefoot   51

Pathfinder Plant   36

Paxistima myrsinites   2

Pea Family
  Beach Pea   22
  Bird's Foot Trefoil   82
  Bog Bird's Foot Trefoil   83
  Gorse   83
  Large-Leafed Lupine   67
  Perennial Pea   22
  Red Clover   23
  Scotch Broom   84
  White Clover   48

Pearly Everlasting   36

Pedicularis bracteosa   78

Pedicularis racemosa   38

Penstemon procerus   62

Perennial Pea   22

Perennial Sow Thistle. See Sow Thistle

Phacelia linearis   69

Phacelia sericea   69

Philadelphus lewisii   41

Phlox Family
  Jacob's Ladder   67

Phyllodoce empetriformis   15

Phyllodoce glanduliflora   81

Physocarpus capitatus   51

Pineapple Weed   75

Pine-Drops   13

Pinguicula vulgaris   57

Pink Family
  Mouse-Ear Chickweed   48

Pink Fawn Lily   19

Pink Mountain Heather. See Red Heather

Pink Pussytoes   5

Pink Rhododendron   13

Pink Wintergreen   14

Piperia unalascensis   45

Pipsissewa   14

Polemonium pulcherrimum 67

Polygonum amphibium 3

Poppy Family
   California Poppy 84

Potentilla anserina 86

Primrose Family
   Broad-Leaved Shooting Star 68
   Scarlet Pimpernel 23
   Sweet-Flowered Androsace 49

Prince's-Pine 14

Prosartes hookeri 42

Pterospora andromedea 13

Puget Sound Gumweed. *See* Gumweed

Pulsatilla occidentalis 32

Purple Mountain Saxifrage. *See* Purple
   Saxifrage

Purple Nightshade. *See* Bittersweet

Purple Salsify. *See* Oyster Plant

Purple Saxifrage 68

Purslane Family
   Western Spring Beauty 49

Pyrola asarifolia 14

Pyrola chlorantha 38

Pyrola secunda 39

Queen Anne's Lace 34

Queen's Cup 43

Ranunculus eschscholtzii 72

Red Clover 23

Red Columbine 3

Red-Flower Currant. *See* Flowering Red
   Currant

Red Heather 15

Red Monkeyflower 8

Red Paintbrush 9

Redstem Ceanothus. *See* Buckbrush

Red Twinberry 40

Rhodiola integrifolia 26

Rhododendron albiflorum 40

Rhododendron macrophyllum 13

Rhododendron menziesii. See Menziesia
   ferruginea

Ribes sanguineum 6

River Beauty 7

Rock Jasmine. *See* Sweet-Flowered
   Androsace

Rosa gymnocarpa 24

Rosa nutkana 25

Rose Family
   Dwarf Raspberry 24
   Dwarf Woodland Rose 24
   Hardhack 25
   Indian Plum 50
   Large-Leaved Avens 85
   Nootka Rose 25
   Ocean Spray 50
   Pacific Ninebark 51
   Partridgefoot 51
   Salmonberry 26
   Sibbaldia 86
   Silverweed 86
   Western Mountain Ash 52
   White Dryad 52
   Yellow Mountain Avens 85

Roseroot 26

Roundleaf Sundew 55

Rubus arcticus 24

Rubus spectabilis 26

Salal 15

Salmonberry 26

Sanicula arctopoides 72

Satin Flower 64

Saxifraga bronchialis 55

Saxifraga oppositifolia 68

Saxifrage Family
   Bishop's Cap 53
   Foamflower 53
   Leather-Leaved Saxifrage 54
   Purple Saxifrage 68
   Spotted Saxifrage 55

Scarlet Pimpernel 23

Scotch Broom 84

Sedum integrifolium. See Rhodiola integrifolia

Sedum lanceolatum 87

Senecio triangularis 76

Showy Jacob's Ladder. See Jacob's Ladder

Shy Maiden. See Single Delight

Sibbaldia 86

Sibbaldia procumbens 86

Sickletop Lousewort 38

Silky Phacelia 69

Silky Scorpionweed. See Silky Phacelia

Silverweed 86

Single Delight 39

Sisyrinchium angustifolium 63

Skunk Cabbage 71

Slender Beardtongue. See Small-Flowered Penstemon

Slender Speedwell 61

Small-Flowered Blue-Eyed Mary 61

Small-Flowered Penstemon 62

Smooth Hawksbeard 75

Smooth Violet. See Yellow Wood Violet

Snakeroot Sanicle. See Footsteps of Spring

Snowberry 17

Solanum dulcamara 66

Solidago canadensis 73

Sonchus arvensis 76

Sorbus scopulina 52

Sow Thistle 76

Spanish Bluebell 66

Spear-Head Senecio 76

Spearleaf Stonecrop. See Lance-Leaved Stonecrop

Spiraea douglasii 25

Spiranthes romanzoffiana 46

Spotted Coralroot 21

Spotted Saxifrage 55

Spreading Dogbane 6

Stachys chamissonis. See S. cooleyae

Stachys cooleyae 20

Star-Flowered Solomon's-Seal 43

Stenanthium occidentale 41

St. John's Wort Family
    Western St. John's Wort 87

Stonecrop Family
    Lance-Leaved Stonecrop 87
    Roseroot 26

Stream Violet. See Yellow Wood Violet

Streptopus amplexifolius 42

Striped Coralroot 21

Subalpine Umbrellaplant. See Sulphur Buckwheat

Sulphur Buckwheat 29

Summer Coralroot. See Spotted Coralroot

Sundew Family
    Roundleaf Sundew 55

Swamp Laurel 16

Sweet-Flowered Androsace 49

Symphoricarpos albus 17

Tall Purple Fleabane 60

Tanacetum vulgare 77

Tansy 77

Taraxacum officinale 4

Thinleaf Huckleberry. See Black Huckleberry

Thread-Leaved Phacelia 69

Thread-Leaved Scorpionweed. See Thread-Leaved Phacelia

Tiarella trifoliate var. laciniata 53

Tiger Lily 18

Toadflax. See Butter and Eggs

Tragopogon porrifolius 59

Trail Plant. See Pathfinder Plant

Trautvetteria caroliniensis 31

Trifolium pratense 23

Trifolium repens 48

Trillium ovatum 44

Trollius albiflorus 31

Trout Lily. *See* Pink Fawn Lily; *See* White Fawn Lily

Twinflower 17

Ulex europaeus 83

Utah Honeysuckle. *See* Red Twinberry

Vaccinium membranaceum 11

Vaccinium ovalifolium 12

Vaccinium oxycoccos 11

Vanilla Leaf 28

Venus Slipper 20

Verbascum thapsis 79

Veronica alpina. See V. wormskjoldii

Veronica filiformis 61

Veronica wormskjoldii 60

Viola glabella 88

Violet Family
   Yellow Wood Violet 88

Water Hemlock 34

Water Knotweed. *See* Water Smartweed

Waterleaf Family
   Silky Phacelia 69
   Thread-Leaved Phacelia 69

Water Lily Family
   Yellow Pond Lily 88

Water Smartweed 3

Western Anemone 32

Western Bog Laurel. *See* Swamp Laurel

Western Columbine. *See* Red Columbine

Western Flowering Dogwood. *See* Pacific Dogwood

Western Mountain Ash 52

Western Rattlesnake Plantain 47

Western Spring Beauty 49

Western St. John's Wort 87

Western Trillium 44

Western Trumpet. *See* Orange Honeysuckle

Western Wake Robin. *See* Western Trillium

Western Wood Anemone. *See* Lyall's Anemone

White Clover 48

White Dryad 52

White Fawn Lily 44

White Mountain Avens. *See* White Dryad

White Rhododendron 40

Wild Bleeding Heart 9

Wild Ginger 2

Wood Betony. *See* Bracted Lousewort

Wood Nymph. *See* Single Delight

Woolly Sunflower 77

Yellow Arum. *See* Skunk Cabbage

Yellow Avalanche Lily. *See* Glacier Lily

Yellow Heather 81

Yellow Monkeyflower 80

Yellow Mountain Avens 85

Yellow Mountain Heather. *See* Yellow Heather

Yellow Pond Lily 88

Yellow Sand Verbena 80

Yellow Wood Violet 88

ABOUT THE AUTHOR

Neil Jennings is an ardent hiker, photographer and outdoorsman who loves "getting down in the dirt" pursuing his keen interest in wildflowers. For 22 years he co-owned a fly-fishing retail store in Calgary, and he has fly-fished extensively, in both fresh and saltwater, for decades. His angling pursuits usually lead him to wildflower investigations in a variety of locations. He taught fly-fishing-related courses in Calgary for over 20 years, and his photographs and writings on that subject have appeared in a number of outdoor magazines. Neil has previously written several volumes published by Rocky Mountain Books, dealing with wildflowers in western Canada, fly-fishing, and hiking venues in southern Alberta. He lives in Calgary, Alberta, with Linda, his wife of over 40 years. They spend a lot of time outdoors together chasing fish, flowers, and, as often as possible, grandchildren.